Craft Handbook for Children's Church

Graded Activities for Ages 3-12

Leslea Stringer
Lea Bowman

BAKER BOOK HOUSE
Grand Rapids, Michigan 49506

ISBN: 0-8010-8197-1

Fourth printing, February 1985

Printed in the United States of America

Contents

New Testament 41

Seasonal Crafts 71

PART 2   Crafts for Primary Students

Old Testament   93

PART 3 Crafts for Intermediate Students

Old Testament 179

8

PART 4   Recipes and Methods

PART 5   Musical Instruments

Introduction

The crafts in this book are divided according to three age groups—Preschool and Kindergarten, Primary, and Intermediate students. The skills and interests of an age group determine whether or not a certain activity is suitable for them. You, the teacher, must decide which crafts your class will enjoy.

The activities in each part of this book are arranged according to the books of the Bible to allow you readily to find a craft for the lesson your class is studying. Seasonal activities and handmade gifts follow the Bible crafts for each age group.

Most of the lessons are simple art projects which fit the theme of a particular Bible story. Thirty to forty-five minutes is enough time to complete most projects, however, some lessons for older children may consume two work periods.

Sections on Recipes and Methods and Musical Instruments may be found at the back of the book.

Plan Ahead

Crafts to fit your curriculum should be chosen at least a month in advance to assure you time to round up necessary materials.

Needed materials can be found in craft stores, fabric stores, school supply houses, and lumberyards. Religious bookstores are a good source for pictures, coloring books, and other supplies. Becoming familiar with these local businesses will save you time in hunting for supplies. Most businesses give churches discounts.

Church members will probably be glad to donate dish soap containers, baby food jars, spools, or any other household items you may need for crafts. In fact, you may want to send a list of needed materials home with your students at the beginning of the church school year. Let people know you are involved with a church school. Someone may have or may run across materials you need.

Planning ahead will also give you time to try out the techniques involved and to make samples to show your students. A sample can be an excellent motivational tool in getting children excited about a project.

The Supply Cabinet

crayons

pastel chalk

rulers

white glue

tacky glue

rubber cement

paste

pencils

felt-tip pens

scissors

18″ × 12″ sheets of construction paper

12″ × 10″ sheets of construction paper

tissue paper

butcher paper

freezer paper

tagboard

sandpaper

typing paper

ditto paper

tape

masking tape

ditto masters

water colors

clear acrylic spray paint

colored acrylic paints

India ink

stamp pads

food coloring

paintbrushes of different sizes

oilcloth for worktables

chenille pipe cleaners in different colors

mailing string (white and brown)

modeling compound

drinking straws

brads

jingle bells

staplers

paper punch

sponges

Bible coloring books

pictures of Bible scenes

coloring books with pictures of animals, flowers, or children

thumbtacks and other hanging devices

Items Donated by Church Members

paint shirts

material scraps

leather scraps

felt squares

burlap

lace, rickrack, gold braid

glitter and sequins

wallpaper leftovers

contact paper

wood scraps

old greeting and Christmas cards

cardboard backings from pads of paper

cardboard tubes from toilet paper and paper towels

wrapping paper

popsicle sticks

cotton balls

frozen fruit juice containers

toothpicks

wine corks

macaroni, beans, peas, and other dried foods

peach and nectarine pits

pop can pull tabs

egg cartons

milk cartons

spools

pill bottles

magazines

sewing and needlepoint scissors

sewing needles

yarn

baby food jars

detergent bottles

PART 1

Crafts for Preschool and Kindergarten Students

Old Testament

1. Creation

Body Pictures

Materials

1 large sheet of butcher paper per child
felt-tip pens or crayons

Procedure

Cut the butcher paper into four-foot lengths. Have each child lie down on a sheet of the paper and draw around his body. Give the form to the child and let him draw in his own features and clothes. You will have to draw in the features for the younger children.

Hang the finished pictures.

Egg People

Materials

egg-shaped containers (Legg's panty hose containers or sugar molds)

self-drying clay   paste or glue
construction paper   potting soil
grass seed   water

Procedure

Make a clay base. Put a depression in the clay to hold the egg. Place the bottom of one half (rounded end) of an egg-shaped container on the base so that it will stand up and be easier to work with.

Using construction paper, cut out eyes, nose, mouth, and ears. Paste these to the outside of the egg half to form a face.

Fill the egg half with soil and sprinkle grass seeds on top. Pat down with your fingers. Moisten the soil and place egg in a sunny place. Keep the soil moist so that the grass will grow. This takes about one week.

When the children come back the next Sunday, they will see that their egg person has grown hair. Send the egg people home on the second week.

Baking Cup Owls

Materials

11″ × 8″ sheets of brown construction paper

paper baking cups

black felt-tip pens or crayons

brads (brass paper fastener)

scissors

owl pattern

Preparation

Before class enlarge the owl pattern and trace around it onto the sheets of brown paper. You will need one for each child. If you have very young children, cut out the owls ahead of time.

Procedure

Have the children cut out the owls.

Mark the eyes, ears, beak, and feathers with a black crayon or felt-tip pen.

With a brad, punch through the center bottom of one of the paper baking cups and the spot on the owl where one of the eyes should be positioned. Open the brad to secure cup. Do the same for the other eye.

Sponge-painted Apples

Materials

pink and green construction paper

markers or pencils

small sponges

small bowls of water

16

red tempera paint

newspaper

scissors

paint shirts

Preparation

Cut out one large apple and a stem to use as a pattern.

Procedure

Lay the newspaper on the work area. Put on paint shirts and mix the paint.

Lay the pattern on the construction paper and trace around it. Draw the apples on pink paper and cut the stems from green.

Dip sponges into red paint and gently dot apples. Do not completely cover the apples. Allow a little pink to show to give the apple texture.

Glue on stems.

2. Noah

Button Turtles

Materials

green construction paper

black crayons

flat buttons

turtle pattern

glue

Preparation

Trace turtle pattern onto construction paper and cut out. Make one per child.

Procedure

Outline the features of the turtles with black crayons. Using small dots of glue, attach buttons. Set aside to dry.

Refrigerator Box Ark

Materials

1 large refrigerator or freezer box	cutting knife
black, brown, and blue tempera paint	1 large paintbrush per child
newspapers	paint shirts
5 or 6 one-pound coffee cans	stuffed animals

Preparation

Obtain a box at a housing development site or from an appliance store.

Cut windows into the sides of the box. If you have a lid on the box, you can make a door out of it by putting several pieces of strong packing tape on the inside, making a hinge. The door can fold up or open from the side.

Mix paint and pour a little into the coffee cans.

Procedure

Provide or have each child bring a large paintbrush from home. Cover the floor area where the children will be working. Make sure the children have on their paint shirts. Put the ark on the newspapers. Paint the main part of the ark brown, outline windows in black and paint blue around the bottom for the sea.

Place the stuffed animals inside the ark. Keep the ark in an area where the children can play with it.

Animal Masks

Materials

paper plates	markers
yarn	construction paper
stapler	fur scraps
paints and brushes	cardboard tubes
crayons	scissors

Procedure

Ask the children to decide which animals they want to be. Begin by cutting holes in the paper plates for the eyes, noses, and mouths. Cut rings from cardboard tubes for the noses.

Paint, color, or use markers to make the faces colorful. Also color the cardboard tube rings and insert them into the holes you have cut for noses. The longer tubes make good elephant trunks. Use construction paper to make other parts of the face such as ears and hair. Fur can be glued around the edges for a lion face.

Staple a piece of yarn long enough to tie around the head to each side of the masks.

Clay Rainbow Pictures

Materials

small paper plates

plaster of Paris or small pieces of wood

tempera paints

clay (five colors)

strong glue

Preparation

If using wood, saw into small, plaque-size pieces, sand the edges, and stain or paint light blue.

If using plaster, prepare according to the manufacturer's instructions. Use small paper plates as molds. Remove plaster from the molds when completely dry.

Procedure

Roll the clay into long "snakes." Put a line of glue in an arch shape across the top of the plaque and attach the first color of clay. Pinch off the excess. Continue in this manner with each of the five colors, placing each very close to the color above it. Other figures may be added such as clouds or the ark and people.

Center the words "God's Promise" below the rainbow, using markers to make the letters.

3. Tower of Babel

Building Block Tower

Materials

scrap pieces of lumber
sandpaper
nontoxic paint
newspaper
brushes

Preparation

Lay newspaper on the work area.
Sand the edges of the wood pieces until very smooth.

Procedure

Mix the paint and give each child a brush and the color he or she prefers. Paint the blocks and let them dry.

When the blocks are dry have the children build a large tower. The blocks may then be kept in the play area.

4. The Patriarchs

Praying Hands (Abraham)

Materials

1 6½" × 7" sheet of pink construction
   paper per child
glitter
glue

small brushes
bowls
pencils and red marker
scissors

Preparation

Fold the paper in half so that it is six and one-half inches long by three and one-half inches wide. With a red marker write the following verse inside:

> I believe in God above.
> I believe in Jesus' love.
> I believe His Spirit, too,
> Comes to tell me what to do.

Be sure to center this.

Procedure

Place the child's hand next to the fold with the fingers closed and the thumb separated slightly. Hold the hand in that position and draw around it. Cut around the line you have drawn.

Apply a small line of glue around the outside edge of the front. This can be done with a small brush or with the end of the glue bottle. Sprinkle with glitter and shake the excess onto a piece of paper. With the marker write, "My Prayer," on the center front.

Tents (Abraham)

Materials

construction paper (light tan is best)
markers or crayons
scissors

Preparation

Draw rectangles approximately eight by five inches on the construction paper.

Procedure

Cut out the rectangles.

With a dark marker draw horizontal lines on one side. Color in the space between the lines. This may be done with one color or with a variety of colors.

Fold the tent in half so that it will stand up. The tents may be used in a sandbox scene.

Jacob's Ladder

Materials

construction paper
glue
scissors
white paper
felt-tip pen

Preparation

Before class cut brown construction paper into strips one-half inch wide and two inches long for rungs of the ladders. Cut other brown strips six inches long for the sides.

On the white paper print or type the song "We Are Climbing Jacob's Ladder."

Procedure

On the left side of a sheet of construction paper glue the two six-inch strips of brown paper two inches apart. The children will be able to measure this by laying one of the two-inch strips between them and then marking that place. Glue on the rest of the cross strips to form a ladder.

On the other half of the sheet of paper glue on the song.

We Are Climbing Jacob's Ladder

We are climbing Jacob's ladder;
We are climbing Jacob's ladder;
We are climbing Jacob's ladder;
Soldiers of the cross.

2. Every rung goes higher, higher.

3. Sinner, do you love my Jesus?

4. If you love Him, why not serve Him?

5. Rise, shine, give God glory.

6. We are climbing higher, higher.

Sandals (Jacob)

Materials

several pieces of heavy cardboard
several pieces of macramé cord

lighter or matches

heavy knife or scissors

crayons or markers

Procedure

Ask the children to place their feet on cardboard while you draw around them. Cut out, using a knife or scissors. Allow the children to color their sandals with crayons or markers. This is optional but will keep the children busy while you are cutting each pair. Punch holes about three inches from the toe on each side and also three inches from the back on each side.

Cut four pieces of cord about eight to ten inches long for each sandal. Tie a knot in one end of each piece of cord. Run the cord through the holes. Adults may burn the opposite end of the cord to prevent raveling.

Tie around the ankle and the top of the foot. These are good to use with Old Testament costumes.

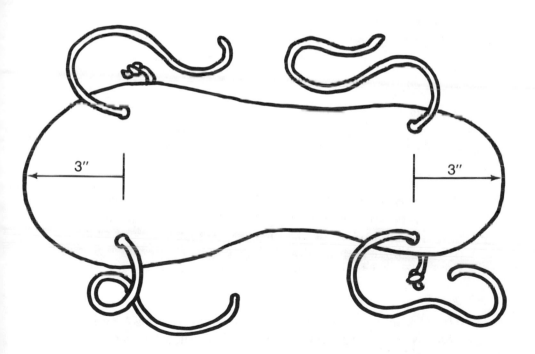

Sack Coats (Joseph)

Materials

1 large grocery sack per coat

scissors

crayons or markers

paper punch

jute or yarn (optional)

Preparation

Gather enough grocery sacks to have one per child. Cut a slit down the middle of the front and a large circle in the bottom of each sack to form the neck opening. Cut a large hole on each side for the arm holes.

Procedure

Give each child a sack and have him draw squares, triangles, stripes, etc., on the sack with markers. Darker colors will work best. Use crayons or markers to fill in the designs.

After the coats are colored you may wish to punch holes in the front and string jute or yarn ties.

Macaroni Necklaces (Joseph)

Materials

large macaroni	scissors
large darning or crewel needles	paper towels
yarn	construction paper
food coloring	bowls

Preparation

Place a very small amount of water in each of several small bowls and add a drop of food coloring. Stir the macaroni in this mixture until colored. Do not leave in the mixture more than a few minutes as it will turn mushy. Drain on paper towels.

Cut the construction paper into small triangles, squares, and circles.

Procedure

Thread needles with pieces of yarn at least fifteen inches long and tie large knots in the end. Start with one of the construction paper shapes so

26

the macaroni will not slide off. Alternate macaroni with shapes until finished.

Tie the ends together and slip over head.

5. Moses

Baking Cup Baskets

Materials
glue and scissors
paper baking cups
flannel scraps
small plastic baby dolls
green construction paper

Preparation

Using the green construction paper cut stems approximately six inches long to look like reeds.

Procedure

Glue reeds to the outside of baking cups, overlapping the ends. Place a small piece of flannel in the bottom of each baking cup and lay the baby doll inside, placing another small piece of flannel over it.

Egg Carton Caterpillars (The Plagues)

Materials

1 egg carton for every two children	transparent tape
yellow or chartreuse spray paint	heavy scissors
several colors of soapsuds paint	eggbeaters
1 black chenille pipe cleaner per child	small brushes
bowls	newspapers
spoons	

Preparation

Cut egg cartons in half lengthwise. Tape together any which might be coming apart. Spray paint the outside of the cup strips.

When the paint has dried, punch two small holes in the top of the cup at one end of each strip. Cut the pipe cleaners in half. Put one of the ends of each pipe cleaner into the small holes. Turn the cup over and round the end of the pipe cleaner in the inside. Use a piece of tape to secure the rounded end of the pipe cleaner to the bottom of the cup. Do this for each child's caterpillar. Curl the ends of the feelers with a pencil.

Just before class mix up the paint (see section on Recipes and Methods at back of book). Cover the worktable with newspapers.

Procedure

Have the children put on paint shirts. Give each child a cup strip and tell them that they will be making a very scary caterpillar. Have two or three brushes for each color of paint. Show the children that they will need only a small amount of paint on the end of their brushes to make a dot or a line. If they have too much paint, it will run and take longer to dry.

The children should start by making big black eyes on the front of the egg cup which has the feelers sticking out. A small mouth can be made with a little bit of red paint. To decorate the body of the caterpillar, paint dots or stripes on each of the egg cups. The children should hold the caterpillars from the underside. When the children have finished, place the caterpillars on a table to dry. The paint will take several hours to dry and the soapsuds will dry puffed up.

The children will be able to take their caterpillars home the next Sunday. The leftover paint can be used to make pretty pictures on scraps of tagboard or construction paper. Again, the paint will need extra time to dry.

Twig Bushes

Materials
small twigs and grass
red and yellow construction paper
glue
pipe cleaners

Procedure

Cut small flames from construction paper. Gather the twigs and grass into a bundle and wrap with a pipe cleaner. Place a small dab of glue on the end of the flames and stick in among the twigs.

Pendants (Crossing the Red Sea)

Materials

small paper plates

yarn

construction paper

scissors

markers

Preparation

Cut fluted edges off the paper plates so that you have a flat circle. Cut a piece of yarn about fifteen inches long. Punch a hole near the top of the paper plate and run the yarn through it. Tie ends together.

Near the top of the flat circle print, "God Sets His People Free." Cut out paper dolls from the construction paper.

Procedure

Using the markers, draw waves on the front side under the saying. Cut the paper dolls apart so that you have three or four holding hands or all separate. Glue the dolls between the waves so it looks as though they are walking through them. You may want to overlap some of the waves. Draw faces and clothes on the paper dolls.

Clay Scrolls (Ten Commandments)

Materials

clay (See section on Recipes and
    Methods at back of book.)

rolling pin

toothpicks

newspaper

Make different colors of clay and put into plastic bags and seal.
Cover the work area with newspaper.

Procedure

Roll out a small amount of clay. Do not make it too thin as it will stick to the newspaper. With a toothpick cut a rectangle. Beginning one-quarter inch from one end place two toothpicks end to end and roll the clay toward the middle, stopping about two inches from the center. Roll the other end in the same manner, leaving a total of four inches unrolled. Make sure the toothpicks stick out.

With a toothpick make an indentation down the middle. On one side print the numbers 1-5; on the other side print the numbers 6-10.

Bake in a slow oven (about 150°) for an hour or dry overnight in the open.

Option

If you wish, instead of coloring the clay, let the children paint their scrolls after they have been baked.

6. Historical Books

Walls of Jericho

Materials

1 large sheet of butcher paper per child

1 recipe of brown finger paint (See Recipes and Methods at back of book.)

paper clips, forks, and various tools needed to make different effects

bowls of water

damp washcloths

newspaper

paint shirts

Preparation

Gather needed materials. Cover the work area and a drying area with newspaper.

Procedure

Give each child a sheet of paper and have him sprinkle a few drops of water on it. Place a large spoonful of paint on each paper and have the children spread the paint around. Have the children imagine a big city on a hill. Let them play with the paint for a while before they create the actual picture.

The city should be built on a hill with a wall placed at the bottom of the hill. Show the children how to use the paper clips and other tools to make a variety of lines. Have them draw in features such as windows, doors, and bricks in the wall.

When finished let the paint dry for several hours. Keep the paintings until the next class session.

Ram Horns

Materials

1 5″ × 7″ sheet of light-colored construction paper per child

3 or 4 cardboard ram horns per child

brown tempera paint

several 4″ × 4″ squares of screen mesh (not too fine)

several old toothbrushes

paint shirts

newspapers

Preparation

Cut the ram horns from lightweight cardboard. Cover the worktable with newspapers and have the paint ready. Be sure to have the squares of screen ready as they are invaluable for making the splattered effect.

Procedure

Give each child a sheet of paper and several ram horns. Have him arrange them in a pleasant design.

When ready to paint, show the children how to splatter paint by dipping their brushes into the paint and shaking most of the paint off. Then hold the square of screen over the paper and rub the brush on it. The paint will splatter below, covering the paper.

When the paper is well-covered, carefully lift off the cardboard ram horns and put the paper aside to dry. The dried papers may be taken home, made into a greeting card, or used for a popsicle stick banner.

Swords and Helmets

Materials

Swords	*Helmets*
tagboard	Clorox bottles (gallon size)
aluminum foil	markers

Swords

Preparation

Draw swords on tagboard and cut out.

Procedure

Give each child a sword and some aluminum foil and have him wrap the sword in foil.

Helmets

Preparation

Clean the Clorox bottles with hot water. Cut off the tops so they are short on one side and curved down on the other.

Procedure

Decorate the outside of the helmets with markers.

Scissors (Samson)

Materials

2 10″ × 5″ sheets of heavy cardboard or tagboard

pattern

crayons

brads

1 large nail

Preparation

Enlarge pattern to desired size. Draw blades separately on tagboard and cut out.

Procedure

Color both blades on both sides. Cross the blades over one another and with a nail punch a hole where they cross. Insert a brad into the front side, then turn over and separate ends.

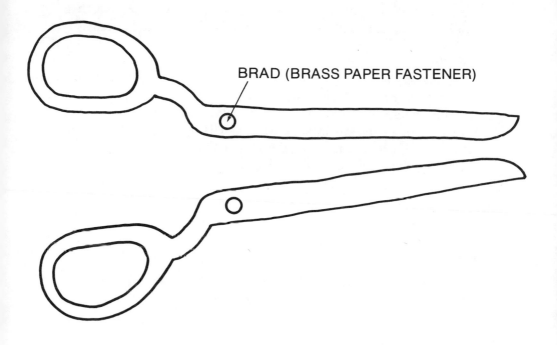

BRAD (BRASS PAPER FASTENER)

Helping Hands Poster (Hannah)

Materials

1 long sheet of butcher paper
blue or black permanent markers
crayons
tape or thumbtacks
newspaper

Preparation

Using a bright marker, write, "Many Helping Hands Make Light Work," across the lengthwise top of the paper.

Procedure

Lay the butcher paper on the floor. Have the children work in pairs. One child will place his hands on the paper and the other child will draw around them. When the first child is finished, reverse the roles. Make sure that the children spread their fingers to make it easier to trace around their hands. When both children have their hands drawn they may then color them. Do this until all the children's hands have been traced.

Option

Lay newspaper over a large area. Have children put on paint shirts and roll up the sleeves. In small bowls mix the paint and then one at a time have the children stick one hand into the color they prefer and then onto the paper. You will need to make sure the paint is fairly thick. The aide can help the children wash hands after each has a turn. This is messier than the first method, but the children really enjoy it.

Crowns

Materials

1 large sheet of yellow construction paper per crown

various decorating items—felt-tip pens, sequins, yarn, etc.

glue

stapler

Preparation

Make one crown to use as a pattern and trace onto the yellow paper. Cut out.

Procedure

Ask children to think about how they want to decorate their crowns, and proceed to decorate. *Suggestions:* Color designs on with crayons or markers, run yarn around the edges, glue on sequins, or draw a design with glue and sprinkle with glitter. Do not decorate the tabs.

Hold the crown up to forehead and measure the length around. Mark with pen and staple at this point.

Star of David Pendants

Materials

any two colors of tagboard

glue

yarn

paper punch

Procedure

Cut two three-inch equilateral triangles. Using these as patterns, let the children trace onto tagboard and cut out.

Glue the triangles together so that one points downward and the other upward.

Punch a hole in the center of the top point and run yarn through the hole. Tie the two ends, making sure that the yarn is long enough to slip the pendant over the head.

7. Wisdom Books

Three-dimensional Corduroy Picture

Materials

1 sheet of tagboard	scissors
light blue corduroy to cover tagboard	cotton balls
glue	crayons
sheep patterns	construction paper
coloring book picture of shepherd	

Preparation

Using the pattern, draw several sheep. Cover the tagboard with the light blue corduroy by laying the material on the table on the wrong side and placing the tagboard on top of it. Turn the edges over and glue down.

Procedure

Have one child cut out and color the figure of the shepherd. Have the other children cut out several sheep. Cut flowers from construction paper. Place the flowers along the bottom of the corduroy-covered tagboard. You may want to use markers to draw in grass among the flowers. Place small dots of glue on a few balls of cotton and glue to the upper part of the

SHEEP PATTERN

picture for clouds. Place the figure of the shepherd in the middle of the picture and scatter the sheep around him. Across the top of the poster print with markers, "The Lord Is My Shepherd."

Burlap Hangers

Materials

10″ × 8″ pieces of burlap	construction paper
10″ dowels	fine-tip markers
gold cording	glue

Preparation

Cut the burlap into the indicated size. Cut the construction paper into six-by-five-inch pieces. On each piece write a verse or two from a Psalm. You will need one for each child.

Procedure

Turn the paper over and spread a thin layer of glue on the back. Center on the burlap.

Fold the top of the burlap over one inch and run a thin line of glue on the backside of the burlap where the fold ends. Hold the folded edge down until secure.

Run the dowel through the casing and tie the gold cording on to each end of the dowel to make the hanger.

Starting at one edge of the burlap pull the bottom string so that the edge will fray. Continue this process until you have a half-inch frayed edge on both sides and the bottom.

8. The Prophets

Paper Chain Prophets

Materials

construction paper	markers
glue	list of the prophets

Cut the construction paper into one-by-four-inch strips. Each necklace will need seventeen of these strips—one for each prophet's name. Write the names on the strips.

Procedure

Put a small dot of glue on both ends of the first strip. Connect the ends. The second strip is attached to the first by putting one end through the loop made by the first strip and then gluing the ends. Continue in this manner until the last strip and then connect the last and the first together to form a continuous chain. Place around the neck as a necklace, or leave the first and last loops unattached and hang up to use as a learning aid.

Finger-painted Fish (Jonah)

Materials

large sheets of shelf paper (must be shiny on one side)	scissors
	stapler
newspaper or other stuffing material	paint shirts
finger paints	

Preparation

Cut large pieces of shelf paper. Mix the finger paint if you are not using the store-bought variety. Lay newspaper on the work area. Put on paint shirts.

Procedure

Wet each piece of the shiny side of the shelf paper and put a small amount of finger paint in the middle. Let the children finger-paint any design they desire. You will have to add a little water and a little paint as they work. Let dry.

When the pictures are dry, fold them in half and cut out two large fish shapes. Staple around the edges, leaving the tail end open. Using the newspaper or stuffing material, stuff the fish from the tail forward until it is completely full. When finished, staple around the open end.

Jonah's Vine

Materials

One 12″ × 8″ sheet of light-colored construction paper per child
several sheets of green construction paper (scraps will work)
green crayons
small bowls of glue
brushes to spread glue

Preparation

Cut out dozens of leaves

Procedure

In the center of the twelve-by-eight-inch sheet draw a wavy line from one end to the other. Glue leaves on each side of the line. Be sure to remind the children that the large end of a leaf goes next to the vine. You may want to write a Bible verse along the top of each child's picture.

Isaiah's Proclamation Banners

Materials

two popsicle sticks per child

1 5″ × 8″ rectangle of cream-colored burlap or light-colored material per child

1 3″ × 2″ picture of the Virgin Mary and the Christ child per child

1 3″ × 2″ sheet of light blue paper per child

blue felt-tip pen

stapler

blue yarn

glue and paste

Preparation

Cut the burlap or material into the required size rectangles. Cut the yarn into ten-inch lengths (one per child). Cut the three-by-two-inch rectangles of light blue paper and print on each, "The Savior Shall Come as a Baby." Buy pictures of the Virgin Mary and the Christ child from a religious bookstore. Gather the rest of the supplies.

Procedure

Give each child two popsicle sticks and have him put a drop of glue at the end of one of the sticks. Press the ends of the sticks together to form one long stick. Set aside to dry.

Have each child paste or glue onto the background rectangle the picture and the verse. One inch of material along one of the five-inch edges should be left free for anchoring the material to the popsicle sticks. Have the children pull out two or three rows of the burlap threads from the three other sides of their rectangles.

Attach the rectangle to the popsicle stick support by spreading glue on one side of the support. Then turn the edge of the material on top of the wet glue. Pat the material down to help the glue saturate the material. Staple the ends of the yarn to the backside of the support to form a hanger.

New Testament

1. Birth and Childhood of Jesus

Napkin Angels

Materials

paper napkins	glue
rubber bands	glitter
fine-tip markers	

Procedure

Unfold one of the napkins and roll it into a ball. Unfold a second napkin and place over the first rolled up napkin. Put a rubber band over the second napkin underneath the ball. This will form the head, neck, and the dress of the angel.

Fold a third napkin into a thin strip and place over the rubber band and pull around to tie in back. Spread this napkin out to form wings. Run a thin line of glue along the outside edge of both of the wings and sprinkle with glitter. Shake off the excess.

With a fine-tip marker make small dots for the eyes, nose, and mouth. You may want to use a yellow marker to make hair or a halo.

Angel Cards

Materials

heavy construction paper or tagboard	paper punch
pencils and markers	angel pattern
shoelaces	rubber cement
ditto master	

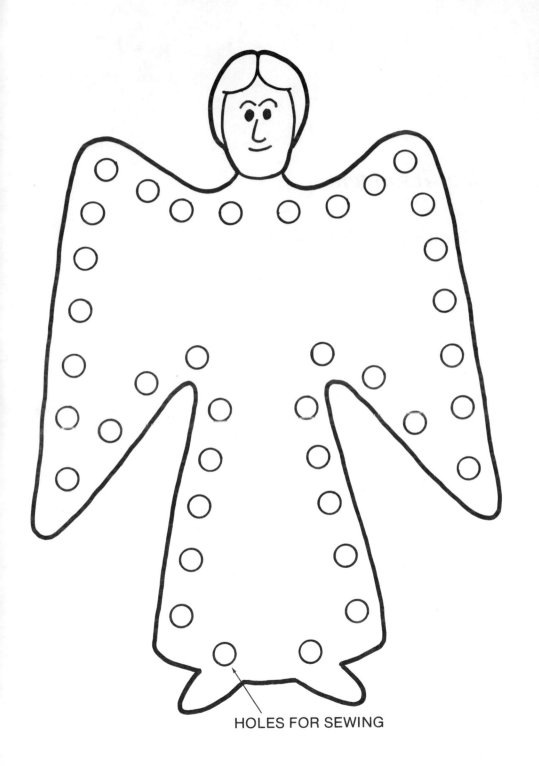

HOLES FOR SEWING

Preparation

Trace the angel pattern onto a ditto master and duplicate.

Procedure

Give each child an angel picture to glue onto the tagboard (use rubber cement). Color in the picture and then punch holes all the way around the outside border. Tie a knot in one end of a shoelace, and, starting on the underside of the picture, come up through the hole and down through the one next to it, and so on. Tie the ends together when you are completely around the picture. At the bottom of the picture with the markers print, "And His Name Will Be Jesus."

Clay Nativity Mural

Materials

1 7" × 8" sheet of lightweight card-board or heavy tagboard per child

1 7" × 8" sheet of white construction paper per child

1 ditto master

1 picture of a nativity scene

white, yellow, blue, and brown clay

moistened cloth

forks and other tools for putting in details

Preparation

Find a simple picture of the nativity and trace it onto a ditto master. Run the ditto off on construction paper.

Glue the dittoed sheets onto the sheets of cardboard.

Mix clay. (See Recipes and Methods at back of book.)

Gather the tools needed to put in detail lines.

Procedure

Give each child a picture of the nativity and demonstrate how to press the clay onto the picture. The children should cover each figure one-half inch thick with the appropriate color of clay, and then apply clay around the manger to look like straw. When all the figures have been covered and the clay straw has been added, have the children use forks and other tools to give the clay the appearance of straw and to add details to the figures. A needle or turkey skewer can be used for fine lines or dots.

When finished, let the clay dry. It should take several days to dry thoroughly. Spray murals with a clear acrylic spray for preservation.

Let the children take the murals home to put in a place where they will be reminded of the reasons why Christians celebrate Christmas. They should be handled carefully.

A larger class mural could be made in the same way. Have each child cover a cut-out figure and glue all the figures to a background sheet. Coat with acrylic spray and hang up.

Sponge-painted Stencils

Materials

construction paper

sponges

stencil pattern of the journey to Egypt

newspaper

colored chalk

paint shirts

black tempera paint

Preparation

Make stencils by tracing the pattern on construction paper and cutting out the inside of the pattern.

Lay newspaper on the work area.

Procedure

Give each child a piece of construction paper. Lay the colored chalk on its side to color in the sky and the ground. Make small bushes with the end of the chalk.

Put on paint shirts and mix the black tempera so that it is fairly thick. Lay the stencil on top of the construction paper picture and tape the sides together lightly to secure. Gently dip the sponge into the black paint and then onto the cut out area, covering the entire open area. Let dry and remove stencil.

Pickup Straws Game

Materials

8 plastic drinking straws per child

transparent tape

1 small plastic bag per child to store
   game

scraps of printed contact paper

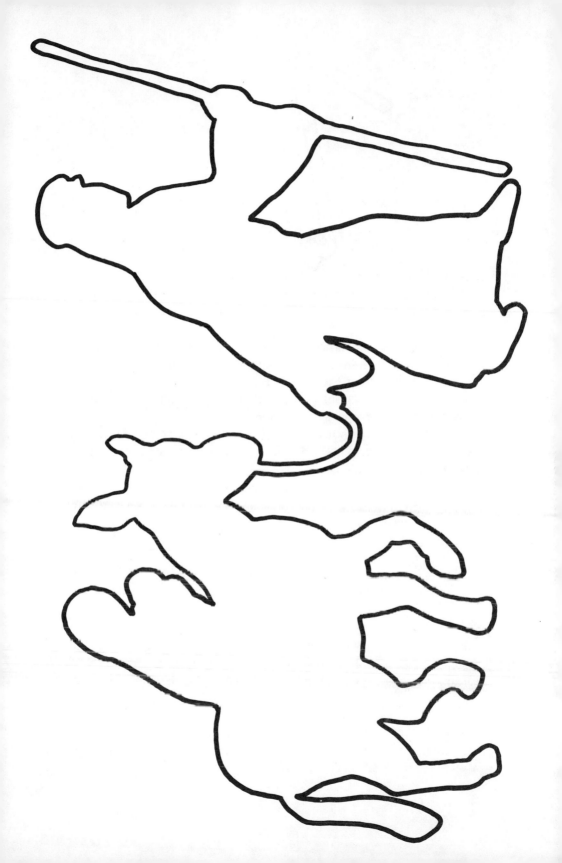

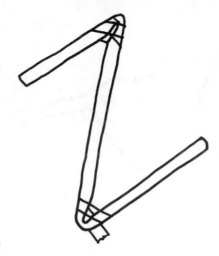

Preparation

Cut out designs, animals, flowers, etc. from the scraps of contact paper.

Procedure

Give each child eight straws. Demonstrate how to bend the ends inward to make a 45° angle. The straws should be bent two inches from one end and three inches from the other. Secure the angles by wrapping tape around the corner sections of the bent straw. The angles may be in the same direction or in opposite directions.

Give each child a plastic bag and let him choose several contact paper designs, flowers, etc. to use in decorating his bag. Peel off the backing and stick the designs to the bag.

When the children are finished, demonstrate how to play the game. Hook the straws together to build as long a chain as possible without breaking it.

Growth Charts

Materials

large sheets of white butcher paper
markers or crayons
yardstick

Preparation

Cut the butcher paper into pieces at least four feet long. On the right side draw a line four inches from the edge for the length of the paper. With a yardstick mark off that area in inches.

Procedure

With markers or crayons have each child draw a life-size picture of how he looks. You may want to have each child lie down on the paper while you trace around him, letting him color in the features. Make sure that the paper is wide enough for the body and the chart.

At the bottom write:

> I'm little now as Jesus once was.
> But I'm growing bigger
> and soon I'll be
> a fisher of men just like He.

2. John the Baptist

Desert Scene

Materials

chocolate pudding paint (See Recipes and Methods at back of book.)

1 10″ × 10″ sheet of waxed butcher paper or finger painting paper per child

several 4″ × 2″ cardboard strips

1 figure of John the Baptist per child (See pattern.)

crayons or felt-tip pens

paste

newspapers and paint shirts

tub of water

combs, forks, paper clips, hairpins

light-colored construction paper

scissors

wooden spoon

Preparation

Make a picture to show as an example.

Before class, duplicate figures of John the Baptist on light-colored construction paper. You also may want to make a figure of a dog to add to the picture.

Mix the pudding so it will be set when class starts.

Cut notches into one side of each of the cardboard strips.

Cover the worktable with newspapers. Also set up a drying area.

JOHN THE BAPTIST

DOG

Procedure

Put on paint shirts.

Give each child a sheet of butcher paper. Wet the paper with a few drops of water. Put one large spoonful of pudding on each of the papers. Have the children paint with the pudding the same way they do with finger paint. Demonstrate the use of the various tools and cardboard strips. After the children have covered the paper with paint, have them start making a desert scene with mountains, palm trees, and low thorn bushes. When the children have finished painting, lay the pictures on the floor to dry.

The worktable should be cleaned. While the paintings are drying, the children can be coloring the figures of John the Baptist and his dog. The older children can cut out the figures themselves. The younger ones will need your help.

When the picture is dry paste the figures onto the painting. If the paint is not dry by the time the children are ready to go home, paste the figures on the next week.

Flying Doves

Materials

glue or paste

crayons or markers

dove pattern

yarn

white construction paper

scissors

Preparation

Cut out the dove pattern and trace onto a folded sheet of white construction paper (one per child).

Procedure

Color the doves with crayons or markers. Be sure to color both sides of the bodies and wings. Cut out the dove and fold the wings on the dotted lines. Glue or paste the bodies together. Attach the yarn to the top part of the body.

The doves may be attached to a hanger or dowel and used as a mobile, or tacked to the ceiling.

FOLD

PLACE ON FOLD

3. Calling of the Disciples

Nutty Boats

Materials
walnuts
white construction paper
toothpicks
clay

Preparation
Crack the nuts in half and clean out the insides.

Procedure
From the white construction paper cut out a triangle two inches wide at the base. Stick a toothpick through the base of the triangle and out again to form a sail. Place a small amount of clay in the hollow of the nut and stick the end of the toothpick into the clay. You now have a little boat with a sail.

4. The Miracle Stories

Mints (Wedding at Cana)

Materials

1 8 oz. package cream cheese	food coloring
2 lbs. confectioners' sugar	granulated sugar
¼ c. butter	small bowls
1 tsp. mint flavoring	newspaper
mint molds (Someone in your church may have these or they can be purchased from a cake supplier.)	waxed paper
	small paper plates

Preparation
Blend the cream cheese, confectioners' sugar, butter, and flavoring together. This will be very thick. Add food coloring if you wish to have different colored mints. Lay newspaper on the work area.

Procedure

Put a small amount of granulated sugar into small bowls and put the mint mixture into other small bowls so that all the children will be able to reach both. On each of the paper plates place a piece of waxed paper (one per child).

To make the mints, roll a small ball of the mint mixture in your hand and dip it into the sugar. Press into the mold and scrape off the excess. Turn the mint mold upside down over the plate and gently press with the thumbs on the sides of the mold. The first couple will probably stick. Put these back into the bowl and try again. Mint making takes a bit of practice but can be done even by preschoolers.

Papier-mâché Trays (Wedding at Cana)

Materials

1 tin pie pan or tray per child (If unable to find enough of these, use the styrofoam trays on which meats and deli foods are packaged.)

strips of newspaper

papier-mâché paste (See Recipes and Methods at back of book.)

oilcloth for worktable

paint

paper towels

brushes

paint shirts

Preparation

If you aren't equipped with enough trays you may get styrofoam trays from your butcher.

Use a paper cutter or scissors to cut a large supply of newspaper strips.

Mix the paste in a large container.

Cover the work area with oilcloth.

Procedure

Demonstrate to the children how to papier-mâché.

Give each child a tray on which to work. The entire tray should be covered with several layers of paper. For the last layer, dip strips of paper towel into the paste and attach to the base structure. Have the children use their fingers to smooth down all seams. Let dry during the week.

The trays may be painted with spray paint or with tempera paint. To moisture proof, spray the painted trays with a polyurethane spray.

Braille Cards (The Blind Man)

Materials

1 3" × 5" card per child   felt-tip pen

1 medium size safety pin per child   ruler

Preparation

With a felt-tip pen write, "Jesus Loves Me," on each of the cards, leaving plenty of space between the letters and an inch above each word. The section above the words should be divided into three horizontally equal rows. The dividing lines will serve as a guide for making the dots of each letter. Following the Braille Letter Chart, mark the dots for each letter on the backside of the card.

Procedure

Pass out a card and safety pin to each child. Have a short discussion about the use of safety pins. Open the pins for the children. Turn over the cards and have the children push the safety pins through the cards at each dot you have marked. When they are finished, the children can run their fingers over the raised dots.

Sample of Revised Braille

a b c d e f g h i

j k l m n o p q r

s t u v w x y z

JESUS LOVES

ME

"Thank You" Posters (Healing of the Lepers)

Materials

large sheets of construction paper
markers
glue
old magazines

Preparation

At the top of each sheet write, "Thank You, Lord."

Procedure

Using old magazines, ask the children to cut out pictures of things for which they are thankful and to glue the pictures onto their sheets of construction paper.

Baking Cup Baskets (Feeding the Five Thousand)

Materials

paper baking cups   scissors
pipe cleaners   ditto master
paper punch   crayons or markers

Preparation

Draw the loaves of bread and the fish on the master and make several copies.

Procedure

Ask each child to write his name on the bottom of a paper baking cup. Punch a small hole on each side of the paper baking cups, being careful not to do it too close to the edge. For handles bend the pipe cleaners and attach to the cupcake holders by putting the ends through the holes and twisting. Put aside.

Color the loaves and fish and cut out. With a black marker make a small eye on each fish. Fill the baskets.

5. Sermon on the Mount

Doily Picture Pendants (Jesus with the Children)

Materials

red construction paper	paper punch
white construction paper	yarn
glue	small picture of Jesus with children
small white doily	

Procedure

Cut the red construction paper in a circle to match the size doily you have. Make a smaller circle from the white paper. Use these for patterns. Have the children lay the patterns on the red and white paper, trace around them, and cut out.

Center the white circle on the red circle and glue. Then glue the doily over both the red and white circles.

If the picture you have of Jesus with children is too large, trim it so that it will fit in the center of the doily. Glue the picture onto the center and punch two small holes at the top of the doily. Run the yarn through the holes and tie the ends, making sure that the yarn is long enough to fit over the head.

"Praise Him!" Poster (Jesus with the Children)

Materials

1 long sheet of white butcher paper or a large poster board 4' to 5' long	scissors
1 picture of Jesus 10" to 12" tall	crayons
1 15" × 12" sheet of construction paper	paste
	felt-tip pen

Preparation

Cut the sheet of butcher paper to the required size. Cut out a picture of Jesus and back it with construction paper. Trim the paper around the picture, leaving a two-inch border. Write in an arch across the top of the poster board, "Praise Him, Praise Him, All Ye Little Children. God Is Love, God Is Love."

Procedure

Paste the picture of Jesus to the poster, centered below the headline. Have the children line up in groups of two. Have one child draw around the other's hand. The procedure should be reversed, so that both children have their hand traced on the poster. Color the hands with crayons.

If you have a very large class, make more than one poster, so that everyone has a chance to have his hand traced.

Pencil Holders

Materials

1 12 oz. orange juice can per child	felt-tip pens
1 9" × 5" sheet of light-colored construction paper per child	wide rickrack
1 snapshot of each child's family	glue

Preparation

Remind each child the week before you do this project that you will need him to bring a large orange juice can and a picture of his family. Have a few extra orange juice cans on hand.

Cut the construction paper into nine-by-five-inch sheets. Also cut two nine-inch lengths of rickrack for each can.

Write across the top of the paper with a felt-tip pen, "Thank You for Making My Family."

Procedure

Give each child a sheet of the construction paper. Have him glue rickrack across the top and bottom of the construction paper. Glue his picture in the center of the paper and then glue the strip around the can, overlapping the edges slightly.

Have the children take the pencil holder home to their parents for use in the kitchen or in the office.

6. Prayer

Popsicle Stick Hot Plates

Materials

popsicle sticks   wood glue or other glue
8″ × 8″ pieces of plywood   black marker
wood stain

Preparation

Sand the edges of the wood and stain. Let dry.

Procedure

Glue four sticks in a square on the wood, leaving about one and a half inches on each side. Fill in the middle of the square by glueing in more popsicle sticks. With a marker write on the center sticks, "Give Us This Day Our Daily Bread," and draw flowers or other designs around the edges.

Put the child's name on the bottom of the front or on the back of the hot plate.

Prayer Plaques

Materials

small pieces of wood	pop can pull tabs
old religious cards	newspaper
decoupage paste	paint shirts
wood stain	sponge

Preparation

Sand the edges of the pieces of wood and stain. Let dry. Burn the edges of the card pictures and verses.

Procedure

Cover the work area with newspaper and make sure all the children put on their paint shirts.

Ask the children to choose a picture or verse. Put glue on the back of each picture or verse and center it on the wood. Pour a small amount of the decoupage paste onto the center of the card. With the sponge gently spread out the paste until the plaque is completely covered. Let dry.

Glue the top part of a pop can pull tab to the back to make a hanger.

7. Zacchaeus

"Jesus Loves Everyone" Poster

Materials

1 sheet of colored tagboard	stencil letters
old magazines	markers
scissors	glue

Preparation

Cut the tagboard to form a large diamond shape. Use the stencil letters to print, "Jesus Loves Everyone," in the center of the diamond shape.

Procedure

From the magazines cut out pictures of all sorts of people. The poster will be better if the children are able to find pictures that show rich and poor and people of all different races. Glue the pictures around the lettering and with the markers fill in the letters. Hang for display.

8. The Parables

Pill Bottle Sheep (The Lost Sheep)

Materials

pill bottles (A druggist probably will donate these If he knows what they are being used for)

pipe cleaners

cotton balls

glue

fine-point markers

Procedure

Place one of the pipe cleaners around the pill bottle near the top and twist on the underside. Bend out about one-quarter inch of the ends of the pipe cleaner to form the feet. Use another pipe cleaner near the bottom to form the back feet.

Glue the cotton balls onto the pill bottle one at a time until the bottle and the tops of the pipe cleaners are completely covered. Use the fine-point marker to make small dots for the eyes, nose, and mouth.

Crayon Rubbings of Coins (The Lost Coin)

Materials

various denominations of coins

crayons

white paper

Procedure

Decide what type of picture you wish to make. The picture will work best if it includes flowers, sky, and clouds. To make a flower, for instance, place a coin under the paper and rub gently with a crayon until the impression appears. Remove the coin and draw in the petals, stems, and leaves and color them.

Mustard Seed Pendants

Materials

construction paper

yarn

glue

mustard seeds

gold or silver rickrack

Preparation

Draw several diamond shapes on construction paper for pendants.

Procedure

Punch a small hole in the top of the diamond and thread the yarn through. Tie the ends, making sure that the yarn is long enough to slip over the head.

With the glue make a thin line around the outside edge of the pendant. Glue on the rickrack.

Put one small dot of glue in the center of the diamond and place a mustard seed on it.

Planting Seeds (The Sower)

Materials

pint milk cartons

potting soil

seeds

water

Preparation

Gather enough milk cartons for the entire class. A school or preschool will have a lot of these. Cut the top off each carton.

Procedure

Lay newspaper on the work area. Give each child a milk carton. Put the potting soil in the middle of the work area and let each child fill his container about half full. Put a few seeds into the soil and pat down. Add more soil to cover the seeds. Water each of the planters and set in a sunny window.

Growing Sweet Potatoes (The Sower)

Materials

1 sweet potato per child

1 clean peanut butter or jelly jar

2 popsicle sticks per child

scissors

instructions for growing potatoes

1 box of toothpicks

packaging string

Preparation

The week before you do this lesson send a note home with the children saying that you will need each child to bring an eight-ounce glass jar.

Buy the potatoes and any other supplies you may need.

Cut four one-foot lengths of string per child. Type up an instruction sheet and duplicate. Plant one sweet potato and make a string holder for growing the plant in the classroom.

Procedure

Give each child a sweet potato and have him stick three toothpicks into the sides of the potato. The toothpicks should form a triangle and will rest on top of the glass jar. Fill the jar with water so that only the tip of the potato above the jar is uncovered.

To make the string holders, glue two popsicle sticks together to form a crossbar. Four strings should be evenly spaced along one of the crossbars and secured with a few drops of glue. Let the glue dry.

Send the potatoes home with the instruction sheet. The potatoes should be grown in filtered sunlight and water should always cover the lower part of the root. When the vine has sprouted, stick two points of the string holder in the jar. Tape the strings to a wall or window so that the vines will grow up the strings.

9. Jesus and the Moneychangers

"Follow the Way" Poster

Materials
5' of butcher paper
black marker
crayons
letter stencils (optional)

Preparation
On the butcher paper center the words, "Follow the Way to Jesus," in large block letters. You may want to use stencils. Fill in the letters with a bright color and outline in black marker.

Procedure
Lay the butcher paper on the floor and have the children put their feet on it one at a time. Draw around their shoes. Let each child have a turn so that when you are finished you will have footprints in a circle around the verse. You may wish to put a picture of Jesus in the center. When you have the footprints on the poster let the children color them in with bright crayons.

10. Passover

Indian Fry Bread

Materials

1 cup flour

1 tsp. baking powder

½ tsp. salt

½ cup water

large bowl

frying pan

cooking oil or lard

rolling pin

honey, jam, or other toppings

Procedure

Mix the first four ingredients. Divide into five or six equal parts and roll until one-fourth inch thick and six to seven inches in diameter. Unless you have an extra large frying pan, fry one at a time in lard or oil at 350°. The result is a light-textured bread that can be used as a dessert when topped with honey, jam, or most any crepe filling.

11. Fruit of the Spirit

Popsicle Stick Frames (Love)

Materials

popsicle sticks

glue

small pictures of Jesus or other pictures that depict love

pop can pull tabs

Preparation

Make an example for the children as the directions are easier to follow when looking at an example.

Procedure

Use four popsicle sticks to form a square. Put a dot of glue on all the ends and glue them together. Two of the sticks will be on top and two on the bottom. Apply two more layers of sticks on top of the first. Set aside and dry after you have three layers. Run a thin line of glue around the edges of the picture. Turn over the frame and glue the picture onto the back of the frame.

Pull off the top part of the pop can pull tab and discard. Glue the bottom half to the top of the back of the frame to form a hanger.

On the stick at the bottom of the picture print, "LOVE," in large letters.

Finger-painted Butterflies (Gentleness)

Materials

large pieces of shelf paper, shiny on one side

pipe cleaners

scissors

paint shirts

newspaper

finger paint (See Recipes and Methods at back of book.)

Preparation

Make finger paint or buy ready-made finger paint. Lay newspaper on the work area.

Procedure

Put on paint shirts. Wet the pieces of white paper and lay on the work area with the shiny side up. Put a small amount of finger paint on the paper and make a design in the paint. You will need to add a little water and a little paint as you work. When finished set aside and let dry.

When the paint is dry cut out a butterfly shape. To get the two sides even fold the paper before cutting.

Punch small holes in the top of the butterfly and push pipe cleaners through each side to form feelers. Cut these to the proper length and twist the ends to secure. Curl the feelers over a pencil.

Hand Plaques (Kindness)

Materials

plaster of Paris

small paper plates

paint shirts

newspaper

gold spray paint

black marker

toothpicks

Preparation

Mix the plaster according to the manufacturer's instructions. Lay newspaper on the work area. Put paint shirts on all the children.

Procedure

Pour the plaster onto the plates. (Make prints one at a time.) Put the child's hand into the plaster and then quickly wash his hand. Use a toothpick to put the child's initials at the bottom of the plaque. When all the children have finished let the plaster dry. When the plaques are completely dry lay them on newspaper and spray paint both sides. After the paint has dried print across the top with a marker, "Helping Hands."

Chain of Love

Materials

old magazines

glue or paste

construction paper

scissors

newspaper

crayons

Preparation

Cut the construction paper into strips approximately one and a half inches wide and six inches long. You will need a lot of these.

Lay newspaper on the work area.

Procedure

From the old magazines cut out faces of people who look like family members or friends. (Some of the children may wish to draw pictures of their family and friends on the strips of construction paper.) Glue the pictures to the construction paper strips.

Glue the ends of one of the strips. Let dry slightly and then run the second strip through the first and glue the ends of the second strip. Continue in this manner until you have a long chain. Connect the first and last loops to form a circle.

12. Gifts of the Spirit

Bookmarks (Faith)

Materials

2 7″ × 2″ sheets of light-colored construction paper

1 bookmark pattern

bright-colored yarn

needlepoint needles

paper punch

felt-tip pens

scissors

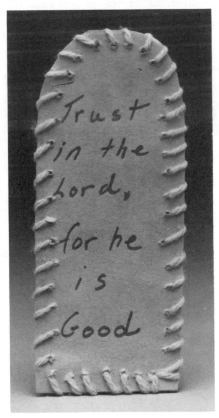

Preparation

Cut two bookmarks per child (see photo). Put the two bookmarks together and punch holes around the edges. Gather the rest of the materials to have ready for the class. Make an example to show the children.

Procedure

Give each child two bookmarks. Cut a length of yarn and thread it through a needle for each child. Show the children how to sew the two pieces together, using a wrapping stitch. When the children have done this, tie the yarn ends together in a small bow. Write along the center of the bookmark, "Trust in the Lord, for He is good," with a felt-tip pen.

Spool Rafts (Faith)

Materials

9 large styrofoam or plastic spools per child

1 yard mailing string per child

1 tapestry or large-eyed needle per child

brown spray paint

2" × 2" squares of red or yellow construction paper

plastic drinking straws

glue

newspapers

scissors

Preparation

Cut the string and thread the needles. Set up a painting area, covering the floor or surface with newspapers. Make an example to show the children.

Procedure

Give each child nine spools and a threaded needle with a large knot tied loosely on the end. Have the children thread all nine spools on their length of string. Remind the smaller children not to push the spools to the end of their string or the spools will fall off. When finished, have the children lay the spools on the table and arrange the spools so that they make three rows side by side. Then thread through the middle row of spools to bring the thread next to the knotted end. Untie the loose knot and tie each of the children's strings with a square knot. Cut off the excess string. (You may have to help younger children with this step.)

Spray paint the top and sides of the rafts. While the paint is drying, the children can make a mast and flag for their raft. Give each child a square of paper and scissors. Have them cut the squares in half, diagonally. Glue the short side of the flag to the top part of the straw. When the raft is ready, slip the straw between two of the spools and anchor the mast to the raft with glue.

The rafts can be taken home and used as bathtub or swimming pool toys.

Picture of Favorite Teachers

Materials

1 5½" × 5½" sheet of white construction paper per child
1 7" × 7" sheet of red construction paper per child
crayons
paste

Preparation

Cut the white and red sheets of paper to the required size. Draw a two-inch frame around each sheet of red paper. Cut out the center.

Procedure

Give each child a sheet of the white paper and have him draw a picture of his favorite teacher. This may be a schoolteacher, a preschool teacher, or a church school teacher. The pictures should fill up the page.

When finished, show the children how to paste the frames to the edge of the white sheet. Have the children take the pictures home or give them to the person they depicted.

13. Communities

Poster of God's Helpers

Materials

1 3' sheet of white butcher paper
magazines
paste
felt-tip marker

Preparation

Cut the sheet of butcher paper to the required size. Draw a long oval circle in the center of the paper. Gather a large supply of magazines which have pictures of men, women, and children engaged in various activities. Firemen, policemen, mothers, builders, and nurses are good examples.

Procedure

Have the children go through the magazines and find pictures of people doing their various jobs. When ready, have the children paste the pictures around the oblong circle. In the circle, you should write in large letters, "These Are God's Helpers."

Hang the poster up in the classroom.

Family Tree

Materials

construction paper	scissors
magazines	crayons or markers
glue	ditto master

Preparation

On the ditto master draw a simple tree. Write, "We Are the Body" across the bottom.

Procedure

Color the tree brown and green, the sky blue, and the ground brown. Cut faces, representing family members, from the magazines and glue onto the tree. Write the names of the people that the pictures represent. The children may want to include grandparents, aunts, uncles, cousins, etc., depending on the amount of space they have.

Rather than using magazine pictures, you may want to draw circles on the ditto master for the children to draw in the faces of their family members.

Another method is to have each child bring a small picture of each family member to class. Cut out the circles you have drawn and place the pictures behind the circles.

Seasonal Crafts

1. Autumn

Leaf Rubbings

Materials

lightweight paper   leaves
dark crayons

Preparation

Gather fresh leaves of various shapes and sizes. The children will enjoy this activity.

Procedure

Choose which leaves you wish to use for your picture. Lay them on paper. The leaves may need to be anchored with small amounts of glue. Make sure that they are arranged so that the sides with the veins are up.

Cover the leaves with a sheet of lightweight paper. Rub gently across the paper with a crayon. The impression of the leaves will make a very pretty picture.

2. Halloween

Sucker Ghosts

Materials

suckers   rubber bands
cocktail-size napkins   blue or black fine-point markers

Unfold a napkin and place over the sucker. Fold down the edges and wrap a rubber band just below the candy.

Use the marker to make the eyes, nose, and mouth.

3. Thanksgiving

Cork Hot Plates

Materials

6″ × 6″ pieces of wood	white glue
scrap pieces of cork tile	wood stain
cork tile glue	small paintbrushes
cork sealer	

small pictures of Thanksgiving items
    such as horns of plenty, fruits, nuts,
    squashes, pilgrims, turkeys, etc.

Preparation

Cut the wood and stain it.

Procedure

Have the children arrange the cork tiles on the wood and use cork glue or white glue to secure. All the wood or just parts of it may be covered with tile, but you must make sure that it is sturdy enough so that when you set something on the hot plate it will not tip.

After the cork is in place use small brushes to put on the sealer. It will dry clear. Let dry and then glue the pictures in the center of the hot plate. (You may want to attach the pictures before you put on the sealer.)

Banners

Materials

1 Handiwipe for each banner

construction paper

markers

scissors

glue

newspaper

dowels or coat hangers

yarn

ditto master

Preparation

Draw a Thanksgiving scene on a ditto master and duplicate. Coloring books are a good source for traceable pictures.

Procedure

Color the picture.

Spread out the Handiwipe on the table. Put a thin line of glue around the outside edge of the back of the picture and center on the Handiwipe. Lap about one inch of the top of the banner over the bottom of a coat hanger or dowel. Staple or glue to secure it. Across the top write, "Thank You, Lord."

4. Advent—Christmas

Advent Wreaths

Materials

small paper plates

green clay (See Recipes and Methods at back of book.)

newspaper or oilcloth

small candles (1 purple, 3 pink, 1 white per wreath)

purple ribbon

Preparation

Mix clay before class. Lay newspaper or oilcloth on the work area.

Procedure

Roll the clay out in long thin pieces. Start on the outside edge of the paper plate and coil the clay inward until the top of the plate is covered. Evenly space the three pink candles and the one purple candle around the plate. Place the white candle in the center. Make tiny bows from the purple ribbon and tie around the base of each candle.

Cup Bells

Materials

heavy paper cups (Do not use styro-foam.)

jingle bells

ribbon

glue

glitter

newspaper

gold or silver spray paint

Preparation

Before class spray paint the outsides and insides of the paper cups.

Procedure

Run a line of glue around the top of the cup and sprinkle with glitter. Shake the excess onto newspaper.

Poke a small hole in the bottom of the cup and run a long piece of ribbon through the hole. Thread a four-inch piece of ribbon through the hole of the jingle bell and tie the ends together. Loop the long ribbon that comes through the cup through the ribbon loop on the bell. Pull the longer ribbon down inside the cup and tie a knot in it to prevent the jingle bell from pulling to the top of the cup.

Make several bells and hang them together as chimes.

Good Deed Mangers

Materials

small boxes (kitchen matchboxes work well)

construction paper

pieces of yarn

ditto master

plastic babies from a craft or dime store

small pieces of flannel

small plastic bags

Preparation

Use a ditto master to duplicate the following note:

Dear Parent,

This is a good deed manger. For each good deed your child does, please allow him/her to place one piece of yarn in the manger. By Christmas Eve the manger should be full and the baby may be wrapped in a small piece of flannel and placed in the manger.

Thank you.

Cut the construction paper so that it is big enough to wrap around the box or cut strips so that the sides can be covered individually.

Procedure

Explain to the children what they are making and what the note says. Use construction paper to cover the sides of the mangers.

Put the flannel, yarn, manger, and the baby into plastic bags for the children to take home.

5. Winter

Cranberry-Popcorn Strings

Materials

popped popcorn	cranberries
thread	small squares of paper
needlepoint needles with dull points	

Preparation

Pop the popcorn the day before class. The popcorn strings better when it is allowed to become stale. Keep the cranberries refrigerated until ready to use.

Procedure

Thread the needle and knot the ends of a doubled thread. The thread should be approximately two feet long. Stick the needle through a square of paper and slide the paper to the end of the thread. This will help to anchor the popcorn and cranberries. Thread on the cranberries and popcorn, alternating them in a colorful design. Encourage the children to use more of the popcorn than cranberries.

When finished, tie several strings together and wrap the strings around a tree or in the branches of a tree. If possible, use a tree that can be seen from inside the classroom. The children will enjoy watching birds eat the berries and popcorn.

Peanut Butter Birdfeeders

Materials

large pinecones

large jar of peanut butter

scissors

large pan

wooden spoon

medium or heavyweight red yarn

newspapers

cornmeal

Preparation

Mix one part cornmeal to three parts peanut butter in a large pan. Cut yarn into one-foot lengths. Cover the work area with newspapers.

Procedure

Working with the middle of the length of yarn, twist the yarn around a pinecone several times. Tie the ends of the yarn together to make a loop to be used as a hanger.

Roll the pinecone in the peanut butter mixture, trying to keep the yarn from being completely covered. Let the cone dry slightly, and hang the feeders in a tree.

Marshmallow Snowpeople

Materials

large marshmallows

cake icing

toothpicks

miscellaneous candies and cake decorations

1 large sheet of colored tissue paper

needle

thread

Preparation

Gather all the materials and make up some examples to show how the snowpeople can be decorated and "dressed."

Procedure

For each snowperson you will need two marshmallows. Push a toothpick through one of the marshmallows to form the base. Push the second marshmallow on top, being careful not to push through the top of the head. If the children are going to eat the snowpeople later, you may want to use cake icing as a bonding paste between the two marshmallows. Use various candies to decorate the snowpeople. Secure the candies to the marshmallows with small amounts of icing.

Examples

Hats: Flat mints may be used for brims and gumdrops for crowns.

Face: Decorate with tubes of cake or cookie frosting. Use a candy corn with the wide end cut off for the nose.

Collar: Before attaching the head to the body, place a flat mint between the two parts. Spread a little frosting around the underside of the mint and put a small drop down the front for the scarf.

Buttons: Apply small dabs of the frosting and sprinkle on decorating beads while the frosting is wet.

Arms: Slide a toothpick horizontally through the second marshmallow to make arms.

Skirts: Use a needle, thread, and tissue paper. Cut a very small rectangle out of the tissue paper and gather at the top by sewing along the edge. Leave some of the thread at both ends so you can tie the skirt on the snowperson.

Send the snowpeople home with the children, eat them, make some hot chocolate and float them on top, or use them to decorate a cake.

Snowpeople Paper Dolls

Materials

rectangular pieces of white paper
scissors
felt-tip pens or crayons

Preparation

Fold the paper like an accordion. Make sure that it is folded into equal sections. On the top section facing you, draw three circles to make a snowperson. One side of the bottom circle should touch the fold. Draw stick arms from the sides of the middle circle. One arm should touch the fold.

Procedure

Cut the snowpeople out being careful not to cut the folded edges of the bottom circle or the arm. Unfold and you have a chain of snowpeople. Using crayons or felt-tip pens, color in facial features and clothing.

6. St. Valentine's Day

Finger-painted Valentines

This lesson should be done the week before St. Valentine's Day.

Materials

1 18″ × 24″ sheet of butcher or freezer paper per child	large spoon
	newspapers
red finger paint (See Recipes and Methods at back of book.)	bowls of water
	paint shirts
finger-painting tools: combs, toothbrushes, paper clips, forks	

Preparation

Fold each sheet of paper in half to make a twelve-by-eighteen-inch rectangle. Draw a half of a very large heart, using the fold for the center point. Cut out and have ready. Make a recipe of red finger paint. Cover the worktable and a drying area with newspapers.

Procedure

Put a paint shirt on each child. Pass out the hearts and have the children open them so that the waxed side is up. Sprinkle a few drops of water and put two large spoonsful of paint on each paper. Have the children spread the paint to cover the paper. Give the children a chance to play with it. Using various tools, have the children see what effects they can achieve.

When ready to make the final valentine, have the children smooth out the paint. Print the name of a special person in the middle of each valentine. The children may want their own name, a parent's or grandparent's name, or the name of a friend. The children may decorate the outside edges as they choose. When finished, put the papers on the drying area until the next week.

Have each child take home his valentine to give to the special person for whom it was made.

Printed Valentines

Materials

1 8″ × 10″ sheet of white construction paper per child

½ potato per child

red felt-tip pen

small bowls of thick red tempera paint

newspapers

paint shirts

Preparation

Cut each potato in half and outline a heart in the center of each. To make an effective printing stamp, the areas which you desire to print need to stand out from those areas you do not desire to print. Cut away all the potato surrounding the heart. The cut-away portion should be approximately one-half inch lower than the top of the heart. You may want to make hearts of several different designs or sizes. Just before class mix the paint and prepare the painting area.

Procedure

Give each child a sheet of construction paper and have him fold it in half lengthwise to make a five-by-eight-inch card. Before the children start to print the outside, write a short saying and print the child's name on the inside of each card. By doing this first, you will not have to worry if the paint is not dry later.

Use a scrap piece of paper to show the children how to use the potato stamp to print a design. Remind them not to dip the potato too deeply in the paint. When finished, place the cards in a drying area until thoroughly dry.

Have the children take the cards home to give to their parents, to a sister or brother, or to a friend.

7. St. Patrick's Day

Tissue Paper Vases

Materials

baby food jars	small bowls
white or green tissue paper	small dried flowers
shamrock or other stickers	paint shirts
decoupage paste or glue	newspaper

Preparation

Cut or tear many small pieces of tissue paper. Pour decoupage paste or glue into small bowls. Put newspaper over the work area.

Procedure

Give each child a jar and show him how to put on the tissue paper by dipping it into the glue. Overlap the pieces until the entire jar is covered. Don't worry about neatness as the glue will dry clear. Let dry.

Place the stickers on the front and put some dried flowers into the jar. (Shamrocks may be made from green construction paper and glued on the jar.)

8. Palm Sunday

Fans

Materials

two small paper plates per child	stapler
popsicle sticks	ditto master
glue	

Preparation

Find a picture of Jesus' entry into Jerusalem. Trace it onto a ditto master and duplicate.

Make sure that the picture will fit on the plates.

Procedure

Glue the ends of two popsicle sticks together. Use strong glue. Color the picture.

Trim the outside edges of the picture to make a circle. Glue the picture to the back of one of the paper plates. You may want to color two pictures and glue to the backs of each of the plates. If not, color or make designs on the second plate. Also color around the edges of the first plate.

Put the plates together front to front. Staple around the edges. Leave about one-quarter inch open at the bottom. Put a dab of glue on one end of the stick. Put the stick into the plates' opening and hold while you staple to close completely. Put several staples close to and over the stick to secure.

9. Easter

Crushed Cereal Crosses

Materials

cereal that can be easily crushed	heavy black yarn
rolling pin	glue
large plastic bags	scissors
12" × 10" sheets of white construction paper	felt-tip pens
	newspaper

Preparation

On each sheet of white construction paper draw a cross nine inches high and seven inches wide. At the top of the paper write, "Bless This Day." Measure the amount of yarn needed to outline the cross.

Procedure

Put the cereal into large plastic bags, seal tightly, and crush with a rolling pin. Draw a thin line around the cross with the glue. Carefully lay the yarn on the line of glue and let dry. Cut off excess yarn. Fill in the middle of the cross with glue and sprinkle with crushed cereal. Shake the excess off onto newspaper. Let dry.

Cross Cards

Materials
construction paper

scissors

crayons

markers

Preparation
Draw several crosses six inches by three inches to use as patterns.

Procedure
Fold the construction paper in half and place the cross with the left arm on the fold. Draw around the cross and cut out, being careful not to cut the fold. Remove pattern and open up the card. On the inside print, "He Is Risen." Let the children color any design they wish on the front of the card.

Tissue Paper Cup Butterflies

Materials
1 9" × 7" sheet of heavyweight construction paper per child

1" squares of several colors of tissue paper

bowls

unsharpened pencils

black crayons

small bowls of glue

black construction paper

scissors

paper cutter

Preparation
Draw or ditto on sheets of construction paper the base for the butter-flies (see pattern). Cut out the butterflies. Using a paper cutter, cut one-inch squares of colored tissue paper. Also cut one-half-inch strips of black construction paper for the feelers. Make an example to show the children. Just before class put bowls of each color of tissue paper and small bowls of glue on the worktable.

Procedure
Give each child a butterfly, a black crayon, and a pencil. Have the children color the center part of the butterfly with the black crayon. This will be the body.

82

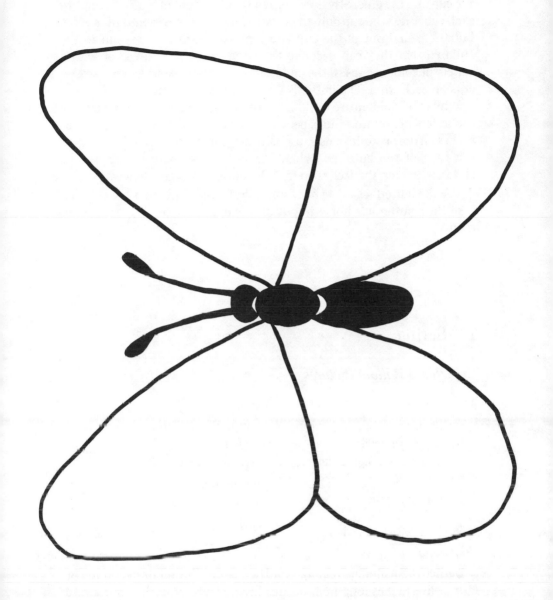

Demonstrate how to cup the tissue paper around the flat end of a pencil. Then holding the tissue paper cup on the pencil, dip the bottom of the cup into the glue. Stress that only a small amount of glue is needed for each cup. Press the cup onto the appropriate place on the butterfly's wing. Lift the pencil out of the cup and repeat the process. Explain to the children that they can decorate the wings with dots, lines, or with a variety of colored cups. If the children tire easily, have them only scatter dots on each wing. The butterfly will look nice this way, too.

While the children are working on the wings, you can curl the ends of the feelers by running the paper over a scissor blade. Leave about three inches on the opposite ends to use as an anchor for attaching the feelers to the back of the butterfly. When the wings are completed, have the children glue on the feelers so that the curled ends face upward.

Use the butterflies for a pretty spring bulletin board or let the children take their butterflies home to put on a window or to hang up in their rooms.

10. Spring

Pussy Willow Pictures

Materials

1 6″ × 8″ sheet of light blue construction paper per child

1 6″ × 8″ sheet of lightweight cardboard per child

5 or 6 twigs per child

1 ditto master and several sheets of white paper

crayons or felt-tip pens

cotton balls

green Easter grass

glue

Preparation

Gather the materials required for the lesson. Cut off or pick up twigs four or five inches long from bushes in your yard or in the churchyard. Find a picture of a bunny or a robin in a coloring book. It should be approximately three inches high. Draw these on a ditto master and duplicate. If working with very small children, cut out each of the pictures. You need one per child. Make an example to show the children.

Procedure

Give each child a sheet of construction paper and cardboard. Have them apply drops of glue on the corners of the paper and attach to the cardboard. Then give the children several balls of cotton and have them pull each ball apart into five pieces. They should roll each piece into a small ball. Set aside when finished.

Draw a wavy line across the page approximately two inches from the bottom with a green crayon. Spread glue below the line and press Easter grass on the glue. On the left side above the grass line, place the twigs in a fan or bush shape. When the placement is correct, glue the twigs down.

While the glue is drying the children can color the bunny or bird. If these have not been cut out, have the children do so. The animal should be glued on beside the bush. Glue the small balls of cotton next to the twigs to form pussy willow blossoms.

When finished, have the children take the pictures home.

Paper Flowers

Materials

popsicle sticks

white construction paper or material

various colors of material or construction paper

glue

Preparation

Cut out a flower to use for a pattern. Draw several flowers on construction paper or material.

Procedure

Put a dot of glue on the top of a popsicle stick. Glue on the flowers.

The children can make several flowers in a short time so be sure to provide plenty of material. You may wish to cover tin cans to use as vases.

Salt or Sugar Flowers

Materials

8" × 4" strips of pastel construction paper

salt or sugar

large and medium brushes

small bowls of thick green, yellow, pink, blue, and white tempera paint

newspaper

paint shirts

Preparation

Cut the strips of paper to the required size. Just before class mix the paint and put it into small bowls. Cover the painting table and a drying area with newspaper.

Procedure

Show the children how to paint a stem which forks off into another stem about halfway up the sheet of paper. Next show the children how to make the center of a flower by loading a large brush with paint and

twisting it around until a circle has been formed by the bristles. Make two circles approximately one inch from the end of the flower stems. The petals are made by pressing a large brush onto the paper, leaving a glob of paint. Two or three petals can be made before you redip the brush into the paint. Leaves for the flowers may be made by dipping a brush into green paint and pressing it two or three times in a straight line from the stem.

When the children have finished painting the flowers, have them sprinkle salt or sugar onto the wet paint. The salt or sugar will adhere to the wet paint but not to the paper. The excess salt or sugar can be gently shaken off just before class ends.

11. Pentecost

Dove Pendants

Materials

dove pattern	markers
red and white construction paper	glue
paper punch	scissors
yarn	

Procedure

Cut out the dove pattern. Trace the pattern onto red construction paper. Cut out. After all the children have cut out their doves, cut the pattern down by one-quarter inch and have them cut a smaller dove from the white paper. Glue the white dove on top of the red one so that the red forms a border around the white.

With the red marker write the name of the child in the center of the white dove. Punch a hole at the top of the wing and run the yarn through it, making sure to allow enough to slip over the head. Tie the ends.

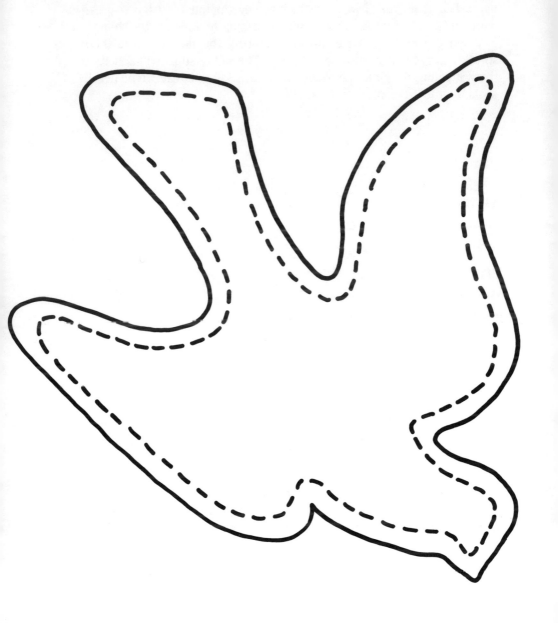

12. Gifts

Cinnamon-Sugar Jars

Materials

markers	ribbon
baby food jars	stickers
spray paint	cinnamon and sugar
newspaper	

Preparation

Lay the newspaper on the work area. Use the spray paint to paint the lids of the jars. Let dry.

Procedure

Carefully fill the jars with a mixture of cinnamon and sugar. Put the painted lids on the filled jars.

You will want to use appropriate stickers to indicate the occasion for which the gift jars are to be used. For example, if they are to be Christmas gifts, stickers of holly or nativity scenes would be best. Flowers or birds could indicate Mother's Day gifts. Put the sticker on the lid.

Cut the ribbon so that it is long enough to fit around the jar and tie in a bow.

With a marker print, "Cinnamon-Sugar" on the front of the jar.

Napkin Holders

Materials (Each child will make four napkin holders.)

2 cardboard toilet paper rolls per child	glue in small bowls
1 yard of colorful material	small paintbrushes
rickrack that coordinates with the material	tissue paper

Preparation

Gather enough cardboard rolls to provide two per child. Cut each in half with a sharp knife. Cut strips of material two inches wide and four inches long. You will need four strips per child. Cut the rickrack into four-inch lengths. Each child will need four of these. Make a napkin holder to show the children. Just before class pour a small amount of glue into several bowls and put in the center of the worktable.

Procedure

Give each child four cardboard rolls and four strips of material. Demonstrate how to attach the material to each of the rolls by spreading a line of glue on each end of the material and then laying the tube on top and wrapping the material around it. Do this for each of the four rolls.

Show the children how to attach the rickrack to the tubes. Use a brush to apply dots of glue to the area where the rickrack is to be attached.

Let the glue dry thoroughly. Help the children wrap the napkin holders in tissue paper as presents for their mothers.

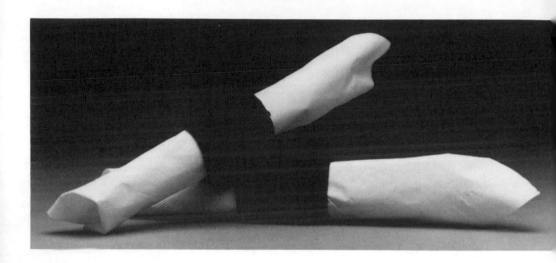

Pencil Holders

Materials

1 6-oz. orange juice can per child	light-colored construction paper
narrow rickrack, ribbon, yarn, sequins, or other decorations	glue
	newspapers
½ potato per child	scissors
several small pans or bowls of thick tempera paint	paint shirts

Preparation

Remind parents in advance that their children will need to bring a small juice can for this project.

Cut strips of construction paper to fit around the cans. Decide what type of edging you want to use around the top and bottom of the cans and buy the required amount. Cut two lengths of edging for each child. Cut each potato in half and make a printing stamp out of each. You will want to use a variety of stamps. Stars, flowers, crosses, small animals, and geometric shapes make excellent stamps.

Before class mix two or three colors of thick tempera paint. Cover your painting area with newspaper.

Procedure

Demonstrate how to print with a potato stamp. Remind the children that a stamp needs to be only lightly covered with paint.

Give each child a strip of paper and have him print a design on it. While the strips are drying, the children may make several pictures, using the potato stamps.

Just before it is time to go, have the children spread a small amount of glue on the top and bottom edges of their juice cans. Wrap the printed strips around the cans. Have the children apply small dots of glue around the cans near the top and bottom edges. Press the edging material to the wet glue and secure the ends.

The children will have a pencil holder to give to a special person such as a parent, brother, sister, or grandparent.

Pencil Holders

Materials
12-oz. tin cans
flowered material or contact paper
glue
scissors

Preparation

Cut the tops off the cans. Clean well. Cut the material or the contact paper into rectangles about ten inches by four inches.

Procedure

Give each child one can and one piece of the material or contact paper. Wrap the material around the can and glue the two ends together. Let dry. If you use contact paper, peel off the backing and carefully wrap around the can, making sure to pull it tight to get out all the air bubbles.

Nut Cup Flower Cards

Materials

colored nut cups	glue
construction paper	yarn
wallpaper samples in solid colors	paper punch

Preparation

Cut stems and leaves from green construction paper. Cut petals from the pastel colors. Cut the wallpaper into rectangles about eight inches by four inches. Cut the construction paper into rectangles seven inches by three inches.

Procedure

Fold the rectangle pieces of wallpaper and construction paper in half. Insert the construction paper into the wallpaper, matching the folds. Run a thin line of glue around the edges between the two pieces. Glue so that the wallpaper will be on the outside and the construction paper on the inside.

On the inside of the card print a message such as, "Happy Mothers' Day, I Love You," and the name of the child. Glue the stems and leaves on the front of the card. Put the nut cup at the top of the stem and draw around it. Remove the nut cup and glue petals so that they slightly overlap the circle you drew. Glue the nut cup in place.

Punch two holes—one at the top and one at the bottom—on the left side of the front of the card. Run yarn through the holes and tie a bow in the front.

PART 2

Crafts for Primary Students

Old Testament

1. Creation

Creation Wheels

Materials

1 large paper plate per child	scissors
magazines with pictures of the sun, moon, earth, clouds, mountains, seas, animals, birds, and people	paste
	crayons
felt-tip pen	

Preparation

Divide each plate into seven equal parts. Use a pencil to mark the divisions. The children will go over the lines with a crayon.

Procedure

Give each child a paper plate. Have him use a bright-colored crayon to trace over the dividing lines. Label the areas one through seven near the center of each.

Have the children go through magazines to find small pictures of things that God made on each of the seven days. Day 1—light; Day 2—sky, oceans; Day 3—plants; Day 4—sun, moon; Day 5—fish, birds; Day 6—animals, man; and Day 7—nothing, for God rested. The pictures should be cut out and pasted in the appropriate area. Make sure that the children do not cover the numbers. If the right picture cannot be found, have the child draw it with crayons. On Day 7 write with a felt-tip pen, "And He Rested."

Creation Place Mats

Materials

15″ × 18″ sheets of construction paper	clear contact paper
1 8″ × 10″ unlined index card per mat	flowered contact paper
scissors	paste or glue
felt-tip pens	magazines

Procedure

On the index cards print, "And it was good." Glue the index cards in the center of the construction paper. From magazines cut out small (three- or four-inch) pictures of things that God created. Paste the pictures on the construction paper in a pleasing arrangement.

Cut two fifteen-by-eighteen-inch pieces of clear contact paper per place mat. These need to be exactly the same size as the construction paper.

To apply the contact paper to each side of the construction paper mat, peel off the paper backing, lay the contact paper on a table with the sticky side up, carefully line up the edges of the mat with the contact paper, and smooth the paper down with your hands. Use the same procedure to cover the other side of the mat.

Cut the flowered contact paper in strips the length of the place mat and one-half inch wide. Peel the backing off and apply one-quarter inch of the strip of contact paper to one edge of the mat, folding the other half over to the opposite side to seal.

Finger-painted Animals

Materials

several colors of finger paints (See Recipes and Methods at back of book.)	black pencils
	felt-tip pens
9″ × 12″ sheets of freezer or butcher paper	small bowls and spoons
	painting aids
newspapers	animal patterns taken from coloring books
paint shirts	
scissors	pins or transparent tape

Preparation

Mix the finger paint.

Gather combs, paper clips, butter curlers, toothbrushes, forks, and other painting aids.

Cover the table with newspapers and put a bowl of water on the table.

Procedure

Have the children put on their paint shirts. Pass out the paper. Have the children sprinkle the shiny side of the paper with droplets of water. Put one or two spoonfuls of paint in the middle of each paper. The children should spread the paint around and experiment with it for a few minutes. Show the children different effects which can be made by using their fingers or various tools. When the children have finished, put the papers in an area where they can be left to dry for a week.

The second week tear out pages of coloring books which have good silhouettes of animals. Try to find a variety of animals. The children should cut out the silhouettes and lay the patterns they have made on the finger-painted paper. Trace around the patterns and cut out the animals. Outline them with a black felt-tip pen. The children can probably cut two patterns from each sheet of the finger-painted paper.

Paper Flowers

Materials

flower patterns	crayons or felt-tip pens
glue	small colored nut cups
white or light-colored construction paper	scissors

Preparation

Cut out enough patterns to have one per child.

Procedure

Trace the flower pattern onto construction paper. Cut out the flower and color the leaves and petals in appropriate colors. Glue a nut cup to the center of the flower. If the nut cup is pulled outward slightly, it will make a fuller flower center. A smiling face may be drawn in the center of the nut cup.

Egg Carton Butterflies

Materials

white shelf paper or butcher paper	finger paints
scissors	stapler
egg cartons (1 for every 2 children)	black spray paint
black pipe cleaners	plastic eyes (optional)
felt-tip pens	transparent tape
newspapers	paint shirts

Preparation

Cut the sides and top off the egg cartons so that you have two rows of egg cups. You will need one row of cups per butterfly. Place the cartons on newspaper and spray paint them black. The first egg cup will be used as the butterfly's head so leave it unpainted. Let dry.

Mix finger paint using the recipe found under Recipes and Methods at back of book.

Cover the table on which the children will be finger-painting with newspaper. Also set up a drying area for the wet papers.

Procedure

Make sure the children wear paint shirts. Give each child a piece of shelf paper. Wet the shiny side and place a small amount of finger paint in the middle. Let the children paint their own designs and place in an area to dry.

Pass out the painted egg cartons and have each child poke two holes in the top of the unpainted egg cup. Stick the pipe cleaners through the holes and curl the ends around a pencil. Secure the ends inside the cup with a piece of tape. Using felt-tip pens, make the face on the end of the unpainted cup. Glue on plastic eyes.

When the finger paint is dry, cut the paper into the shape of wings and staple onto the egg carton body. You may want to add a piece of yarn to the top of the body.

Paper Plate Snakes

Materials

large paper plates	scissors
small jingle bells	markers
small scraps of red material	fine metal wire

Procedure

Draw a dot in the center of the paper plate. Draw a spiral from the dot to the outside of the plate. Cut along the lines to form a snake.

At one end use a marker to make a small eye. Cut a small piece of red material and glue it under the eye to make a tongue.

On the opposite end of the snake poke two small holes with a straight pin about one-half inch from the end. Put one end of the wire through each of the small holes and attach a bell. Twist the ends of the wire to secure the bell and cut off the excess.

Use markers to draw designs on the snake.

2. Noah

Animal Mobiles

Materials

2 coat hangers	glue
construction paper	scissors
pictures of animals from coloring books	yarn
old magazines (optional)	tissue paper

Preparation

Slide one coat hanger through another and tape the tops so that the ends are pointed in four different directions. Cut narrow strips of tissue paper in the colors of a rainbow and the length of a coat hanger.

Procedure

Take one of the strips of tissue paper and run a thin line of glue along one side. Place the edge of another strip on the glue. Continue in this manner until all the strips are glued together to make a rainbow.

Glue, tape, or staple the tissue paper rainbow across the top of one of the coat hangers. Trim away excess tissue paper. Set aside.

Cut pictures of animals from coloring books, color them, mount them on construction paper, and cut out them again. Or cut pictures of animals from magazines and mount them on construction paper cut into various shapes.

Poke a small hole in the top of the construction paper animals and thread a piece of yarn through it. The pieces of yarn should be various lengths. Tie the yarn to the coat hangers. Hang up the mobile.

India Ink Scratch Pictures

Materials

1 sheet of 8″ × 11″ tagboard per child	crayons
black India ink	brushes
various objects to use for scratching— paper clips, bobby pins, keys, etc.	newspaper

Preparation

Before class cut the tagboard into eight-by-eleven-inch sheets. Spread newspaper.

Procedure

On the sheets of tagboard heavily color horizontal lines in the colors of the rainbow. Start with reds, oranges, and yellows, and work down to greens, blues, and purples.

When you are finished coloring, cover the tagboard with India ink. Paint the board twice to insure that the surface will be entirely black. Let dry for about five minutes.

Scratch in Mount Ararat and the ark. Add water, bushes, and trees. Scratch clouds or a sunrise in the sky and add a small bird or two.

3. Tower of Babel

Toothpick Towers

Materials

construction paper
flat toothpicks
glue
markers

Procedure

On construction paper draw the lines of a tower. Put glue along the lines and place toothpicks on the glue. Work from bottom to top, making the bottom larger. You will want to break some of the toothpicks to fit the structure. Let dry.

4. Patriarchs

Picture of Abraham

Materials

coloring book figure of Abraham
ditto master
package of stick-on stars
black construction paper

colored construction paper
glue
scissors
crayons or markers

Preparation

Before class trace the figure of Abraham onto a ditto master and run off.

Procedure

Color in the figure of Abraham.

From a piece of construction paper cut a rectangle four inches by two inches. Draw stripes on the rectangle and fold it in half to form a tent. Fold up one-quarter inch from each edge to form a base.

From the green construction paper cut the top of a palm tree. From the brown paper cut a trunk for the tree.

Glue Abraham to the left side of the black construction paper. Put a dab of glue on each base of the folded tent and attach it in the center of the picture. Glue the tree next to the tent. Lick the stars and scatter them across the upper part of the black construction paper.

Altars (Abraham and Isaac)

Materials

altar pattern
brown construction paper
markers
brown or colored tape

Procedure

Cut out the pattern and trace it onto brown construction paper. Fold on the dotted lines and tape the sides together with brown tape if you want the tape to blend in or with colored tape if you want it to become part of the design on the altar. Use markers to draw the chi-rho on the front of the altar.

Wallpaper Coats (Joseph)

Materials

1 8″ × 11″ sheet of tagboard per child	brushes
ditto master or carbon paper	bowls
scraps or samples of wallpaper	pencils
scissors	crayons or colored chalk
glue	

Preparation

On a ditto master draw a large picture of Joseph wearing his coat. Coloring books are sometimes helpful in obtaining a basic design. Duplicate the picture.

Obtain wallpaper samples from a wallpaper store. Cut the samples into strips one-half inch wide.

Procedure

Have bowls of glue and brushes ready. Give each child a sheet of tagboard and have him glue on the picture of Joseph. Lay a strip on the

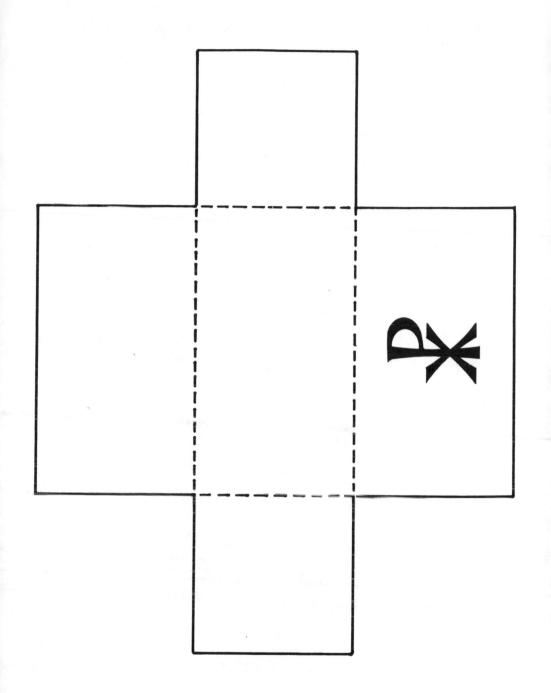

coat pattern, mark the correct length with a pencil, and cut off the excess wallpaper.

Use an assortment of strips, mixing up the designs. Measure and cut all the strips first. Then paint glue on a small area of the coat. The wallpaper strips should be pasted immediately after the glue is applied. If the wallpaper is pre-pasted, just dip each strip into a small bowl of water, blot it on a paper towel, and put it on the picture.

When the coat is finished, decorate the rest of the picture with crayons, colored chalk, or water colors.

Chariots (Joseph)

Materials

cardboard tubes from toilet tissue

masking tape

gold and brown spray paint

small amount of bread dough or clay

toothpicks

tagboard

Procedure

(Use the picture as a reference.)

Cut the top of the tube down on one side. Cut two three-inch circles from tagboard. Place the tube on the tagboard and draw around the end that is not cut down. Cut out this circle and tape it to the bottom of the tube. Punch a small hole in the center of each of the three-inch circles. Lay the circles and the tube on newspaper and spray paint the circles brown and the tube gold. Let dry.

Poke a toothpick through one of the circles and then through the bottom part of the tube. Attach the other circle to the other side of the tube. Place a small ball of bread dough or clay on the ends of the toothpick to hold the wheels onto the tube.

Keys (Joseph)

Materials

brightly colored tagboard	fine-tip markers
heavy scissors	yarn

Preparation

Before class draw a set of keys for each child on the tagboard. These will need to be approximately twelve inches long.

Procedure

Carefully cut out the keys. Across the top or down the front of each key write a Scripture verse. Cut out a circle at the top of each key and string yarn through it. Tie the ends.

5. Moses

Toothpick Basket Pictures

Materials

toothpicks	glue
pictures of baby Moses in a basket	ditto master
small pieces of flannel	crayons or markers

Preparation

Find a picture of baby Moses in a basket floating in the river. Trace the picture onto a ditto master and duplicate it.

Procedure

Have each child color the entire picture except for the basket. Break toothpicks so that they are the same length as the basket is wide. Glue the toothpicks around the edge of the basket, then fill in the middle with more toothpicks. Fold a small piece of flannel and place it at the top of the toothpicks so that it appears to be almost covering the baby.

Water Color Burning Bush

Materials

1 sheet of white construction paper per child	crayons
	glue
water colors and brushes	ditto master
pencils	ditto paper
coloring book figure of Moses	newspaper

Preparation

Trace a coloring book figure of Moses onto a ditto master and duplicate. Spread newspaper over the work area.

Procedure

Cut out and color the picture of Moses. Glue the picture onto the left side of a sheet of white construction paper.

Use a pencil to sketch in a burning bush near the center. Use water colors to paint bright red, yellow, and orange flames. The children may also want to use the water colors to fill in the background.

Wet Chalk Pictures (Crossing the Red Sea)

Materials

1 10″ × 12″ sheet of butcher paper or white construction paper per child

pastel chalk

coloring book picture of Moses crossing the Red Sea

several sheets of various colors of construction paper

2 or 3 bowls of water and sponges

newspapers

scissors

paste

The idea of this picture is to show the Israelites going through a tunnel of water. By using the wet chalk method, the blue chalk used to make the water will have a fuzzy appearance. This makes the water look as if the wave is breaking. Refer to the instructions for the wet chalk method under Recipes and Methods at back of book.

Preparation

Find a picture of Moses and the Israelites crossing the Red Sea. Draw the basic outline of the walls of the wave on each sheet of white paper.

Fold the colored construction paper into a fan to make paper dolls three inches high and two inches wide. Two or three sets of dolls can be made from each folded paper. Cut apart the dolls.

Procedure

Give each child a sheet of the white paper and have him slightly wet it with a sponge. Show the children how to color the wave with the blue chalk. Color just below the crest of the wave and then use a finger to blend the chalk downward to make the wall of the wave. The crest of the wave should be colored with white or cream-colored chalk and blended into the wall. Use brown chalk to color the pathway formed between the two walls. Rub the color sideways to even out the coloring along the pathway. If the paper becomes too dry, wet the dry area with a moist sponge. Lay the papers aside to dry.

Have the children paste on the paper dolls to look like a large crowd coming down the path.

Commandment Bookmarks

Materials

construction paper

yarn

darning or crewel needles

fine-tip markers

clear contact paper (optional)

scissors

Procedure

Fold the construction paper. Draw a tablet that is straight on the bottom and sides and curved on the top. Place one side on the fold and cut out the tablet. Choose one of the Ten Commandments and simplify it. Print the commandment in the center of the tablet.

If you wish to make the bookmarks stronger, lay the tablet on clear contact paper after peeling off the backing. Turn over the marker and do the same to the backside. Cut off the excess contact paper.

Thread a needle with yarn and whipstitch all around the bookmarks.

Paper Scrolls

Materials

long sheets of white paper

two dowels

tape

Procedure

Saw the dowels four inches longer than the paper is wide. Tape the ends of the paper to the dowels, leaving two inches on each end of the dowels.

Print the Ten Commandments on the paper. Roll the paper around the dowels evenly so that they will meet in the middle. Wrap with a rubber band until the paper rolls by itself.

6. Historical Books

Jericho Scene in a Box

Materials

4 large shoe boxes (or one per group)	brown and blue tempera paint
sugar cubes	Easter grass, dried grass, twigs
scraps of construction paper	scraps of material
felt-tip pens	glue dough (See Recipes and Methods
toothpicks	at back of book.)
tan or brown chenille pipe cleaners	cotton balls
scissors	glue
brushes	clay

Preparation

Gather the materials needed for making the box scenes. Obtain a short story of Joshua and the battle of Jericho to read to the children.

Mix the paint just before class. Lay out the materials on the table.

Procedure

Read the story of Joshua and the battle of Jericho to the class. Discuss the story and have the children start thinking about how they would depict the scene. When several ideas have been proposed, divide the class into four groups. Let each group plan whether they want to make the city of Jericho as a fortress with Joshua marching around it or the city after the walls have fallen down and the armies are fighting. Give each group a shoe box and show them the available materials.

Sugar cubes can be used to build the walls and the buildings of the city. Glue them together and paint them brown with a light coat of tempera paint or with felt-tip markers.

Pipe-cleaner people can be made for soldiers. A face can be made from a paper circle and then the eyes, nose, and mouth drawn on with a felt-tip pen. Glue the face to the front of the head. Make hair from a scrap of paper or yarn. Make a tunic by tracing a rectangle onto a folded scrap of material. Place one of the short sides on the fold. Cut out and put a hole in the middle of the folded edge. Slip the tunic over the figure. By placing a few drops of glue on the inside of the material and pressing the two pieces together, the tunic will hold together. The feet of the figure should be placed in a small lump of clay. (Further tips can be found on pp. 131-33.)

Ram horns and shields can be fashioned out of the glue dough.

Swords can be made from toothpicks.

Background scenery can be painted on the back of the shoe box. Use cotton balls for clouds. Dried grass, twigs, Easter grass, and paint can be used to fashion the foreground scenery.

Assemble the box scenes, using glue to secure the people, buildings, and the wall to the shoe box.

Display the box scenes in a prominent place. The children will be very proud of them.

Swords

Materials

tagboard

aluminum foil

scissors

Procedure

Cut out swords from tagboard. Carefully cover the swords with foil. Roll the ends of the foil together on the back of the sword and smooth it with your hands.

Ox Grinding Wheels (Samson)

Materials

1 6-oz. frozen juice container per child	brown tempera paint
several sheets of cardboard	1 ball of brown mailing string
2 popsicle sticks per child	1 ice pick or wooden punch
glue	transparent tape
1 sheet of white construction paper per child	scissors
	brushes
brown crayons	

Preparation

Have each of the children bring a juice container from home. Gather the rest of the materials.

Mix the tempera paint before class and prepare a painting area.

Make an example to show the children.

110

Procedure

Trace around the end of a juice can on a piece of cardboard. Cut out the circle.

Break the popsicle sticks in half and glue them to the cardboard circle as if to mark the quarter hour positions on a clock.

Cut four three-inch lengths of string for each child. The children should place the cardboard circle on top and the sticks underneath and glue each of the strings to the ends of the popsicle sticks. Make small loops with the free ends of the strings as if they are yokes for oxen. When the glue has dried, the entire turnstile should be painted with brown paint.

Give each child a sheet of white paper and have him mark the height of his can on the paper. This will be the width of the strip of paper needed to go around the can. Cut out the strip and measure the required length by wrapping the paper around the can. Cut off any excess. Before gluing the paper to the can, have the children draw stones over the entire sheet of paper with brown crayons. Dot the back of the paper with several drops of glue and wrap the paper around the can.

To assemble the ox grinding wheel, punch a hole in the center of the bottom of the can. Then punch a hole in the center of the turnstile. Stick a brad through the top of the turnstile and then into the can. Fold the arms of the brad back. Anchor the brad with tape.

Ark

Materials

1 12″ × 8″ sheet of light blue construction paper per child

1 12″ × 10″ sheet of yellow or gold construction paper per child

ditto of pattern pieces

several extra sheets of yellow or gold construction paper

yellow yarn

pencils

scissors

red and black fine-tip, felt-tip pens

stapler

rulers

rubber cement

Preparation

Trace the ark angels onto a ditto master. You should be able to put two or three on a ditto. Run the ditto off on yellow or gold construction paper.

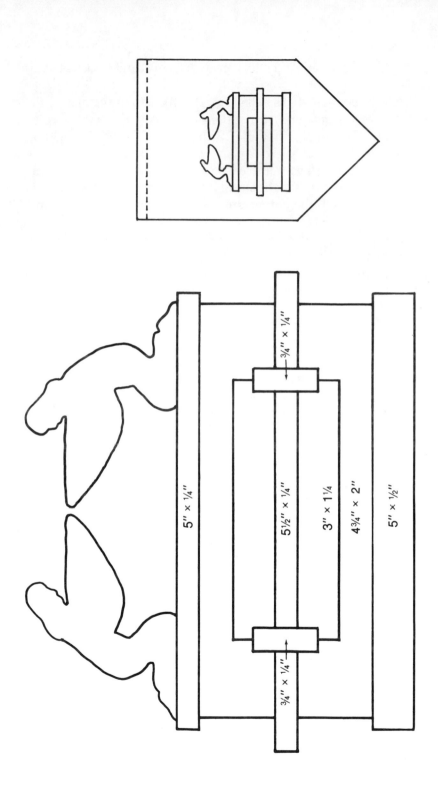

5" × ¼"

¾" × ¼"

5½" × ¼"

3" × 1¼

4¾" × 2"

5" × ½"

¾" × ¼"

Draw each of the different pieces needed to make the ark on a ditto and run them off onto yellow construction paper.

Make an example to show the children.

Procedure

Give the children each a complete set of pieces to make an ark. Have the children cut out the pieces. Give each a sheet of light blue paper and have him find the middle of the width of the paper. This point should be marked at the bottom of the sheet. On each side the child should measure and mark a point four inches from the bottom. Lines should be drawn from each side point to the middle point. Cut along the lines to form the bottom of the banner. Fold the top of the banner underneath one-half inch.

Lay the ark in the middle of the banner. The large rectangle should be laid down first, then the angels directly above the rectangle. Place the five-by-one-fourth-inch strip on the top of the rectangle. Place the five-by-one-half-inch strip on the bottom of the rectangle. Center the smaller rectangle in the middle of the larger one. Lay the last strip across the center of the smaller rectangle. The last two pieces are laid on each side of the small rectangle, covering the horizontal strip. When the children have the pieces positioned correctly they should glue them down to the banner.

Use a black felt-tip pen to outline the angels and the pieces of the ark. Using a red pen, write, "The Ark of the Covenant," in an arch at the top of the banner. Staple the ends of a length of yarn to each side of the banner. The banners can be hung on a wall or door.

Sack Puppets of Samuel and Eli

Materials

2 white lunch sacks per child	crayons
1 sheet of black and 1 sheet of gray construction paper per child	paste
	scissors
scraps of red, blue, black, and pink construction paper	

Preparation

Make an example to show the children.

Procedure

Give each child a lunch sack and demonstrate how to make sack puppets. The bottom should be used for the face of the puppet. The eyes should be positioned in the center. Use two brown dots for the nose. Place a smile on the lower edge. In the fold of the sack, a long red oval may be placed from the smile down. Bangs may be cut and placed across the top part of the sack. Long hair may be cut and pasted on the back portion of the sack. Color the bottom to look like a cloak.

Samuel's hair should be black and his face should have a youthful appearance. Eli should have gray hair and a haggard look.

When finished, have the children use the puppets to perform the parts of Eli and Samuel.

Cardboard Church

Materials

white poster board

large refrigerator or stove box

spray paint

knife

construction paper

tissue paper

Procedure

Spray paint the outside of the box.

Cut out the windows and the doors, leaving them attached along one side. Paint on doorknobs.

Tear the colored tissue paper in pieces and glue them to the windows in a stained glass pattern. If desired, outline the windows and doors with spray paint.

Cut the white poster board into three triangles and staple or glue them together to form a steeple. Cut a cross from gold paper and glue to the middle of the steeple. Attach the steeple to the top of the box.

Papier-mâché Coin Collectors

Materials

1 oval balloon per child

several cardboard tubes from paper towels or wrapping paper

masking tape

strips of newspaper

oilcloth to cover worktable

paint shirts

1 can of cream or light yellow spray paint

1 bowl of rust or brown tempera paint

brushes

1 recipe of papier-mâché paste

paper towels

Preparation

Gather the materials needed.

Blow up the balloons and tie securely. The balloons should be eight to ten inches in diameter. Use a paper cutter to cut a large supply of strips of newspaper. Mix the papier-mâché paste according to the directions found under Recipes and Methods at back of book.

Cut the cardboard rolls into one-inch sections (two sections per child). Cover the worktable with oilcloth.

Procedure

Give each child a balloon and two cardboard rings. Each should tape a ring to the top and bottom of his balloon. Review the procedure of how to papier-mâché. Have the children apply four to five layers of paper on the balloon. Lay several layers of paper across the bottom of one of the tube rings to seal it. Leave the other tube ring open to form an opening. Use a final layer of strips or pieces of paper towels to make a smooth surface. Let the papier-mâché structures dry during the week.

Use a needle or sharp object to pop the balloon. Spray paint the coin collector with a light color of paint. When the paint is dry, the top and bottom rings can be painted with rust or brown tempera paint. If desired, a simple design can be painted on the container.

Explain to the children that clay containers of this nature were used in Jewish temples to collect the offerings that the people gave. When they were full the collectors were broken and the money was used for running the temple.

Collectors can be taken home and used as coin banks.

Purim Rattles (Esther)

Materials

1 spice box per rattle (Tin spice boxes with plastic lids are very suitable.)

dried peas or beans

white wrapping paper

2 2" squares of yellow construction paper per rattle

transparent tape

1 popsicle stick per rattle

glue

scissors

pencils

sharp knife

tagboard

During Bible times the Hebrew people celebrated a Festival of Purim. This was a celebration of thanks for Queen Esther, who saved the Jewish people from annihilation.

Preparation

Measure the size of the sheet of paper needed to wrap a spice box. Cut out enough sheets of wrapping paper to have one for each child. Cut out the yellow construction paper squares. Make two or three small equilateral triangle patterns out of tagboard. The triangles should fit within the two-inch-by-two-inch squares of construction paper. (The triangles will be used to make six-point stars.)

Take the plastic top off of each spice box. Cut a small slit in the middle of the top with a sharp knife. The slit should be slightly larger than the popsicle stick. Put the popsicle stick into the plastic top with about one inch on the inside of the lid. To secure the stick spread white glue around the slit and anchor with a piece of tape. Let dry.

Procedure

Using a pattern, draw one triangle on each yellow construction paper square. Cut out. Also carefully cut out the center of the triangles so that one-fourth inch remains on all sides of the triangle.

Put a few beans or peas into the spice boxes. Attach the lids. Wrap the spice boxes, using tape or glue to secure the paper to the box. Fold the paper so that it fits neatly around the handle. You may have to snip a few places around the handle to make the paper lie flat.

When the wrapping is finished, use the two triangles to make a star of David. Put the triangles together so that the triangles are facing opposite directions (see diagram). Glue the star onto the front of the Purim rattle. Let the rattle dry thoroughly before shaking.

7. Wisdom Books

Book Ends and Doorstops

Materials	*Optional Materials*
bricks	decals
colored felt	rickrack
colored poster board	colored macramé cord
scissors	paint and brushes
markers	glitter
glue	
enamel paint	

Procedure

Clean the bricks well. Paint with enamel paint or cut the felt to size and cover the bricks, using glue to secure the felt.

While the bricks are drying, cut a piece of poster board a little smaller than one side of a brick. Print a verse from Proverbs on the poster board and glue it to the brick.

The other sides of the brick may be decorated with any of the optional materials listed above.

8. The Prophets

Jonah and Whale Silhouettes

Materials

black construction paper	crayons or markers
white construction paper	ditto master
glue	ditto paper
scissors	whale pattern
coloring book picture of male figure (not over 3″ high)	

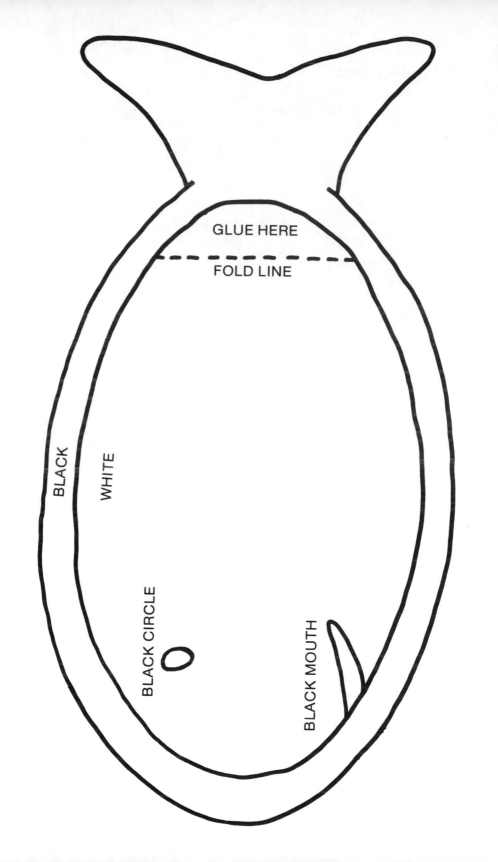

GLUE HERE

FOLD LINE

BLACK

WHITE

BLACK CIRCLE

BLACK MOUTH

Preparation

Cut out the whole pattern. Trace around the outside outline of the whale on black construction paper and around the inside outline on white paper. Make several of these to use as patterns.

Trace the coloring book figure of Jonah onto a ditto master and duplicate it.

Procedure

Give each child a sheet of black and a sheet of white construction paper. Trace around the patterns and cut out. Mark the fold line.

Color and cut out the figure of Jonah. Glue the figure to the center of the black whale pattern. Fold the white pattern about one inch from the end as indicated. Put a small amount of glue on the folded end and attach it to the black pattern so that the white part will fold open to reveal the figure inside.

Cut out an eye and a mouth from the black scraps and glue to the front of the white pattern.

Finger-painted Fish (Jonah)

Materials

finger paint or soapsuds paint (See Recipes and Methods at back of book.)

scissors

stapler

1 18" × 24" sheet of white shelf paper (must be slick on one side) per child

scrap paper

Procedure

Wet the slick side of the shelf paper and let the children finger-paint it. Let dry.

Fold the paper in half and cut out the shape of a fish so that you have two fish.

Staple the edges together leaving one end open.

Stuff the inside with scrap paper and then finish stapling it closed.

Fish Mobile (Jonah)

Materials

yarn	finger paint
4 dowels	scissors
shelf paper	stapler
newspaper	

Procedure

Follow the instructions for finger-painted fish found on page 119, but make the fish only four inches long.

Cross two dowels to form an X and tape in the middle. Tie one end of a piece of yarn around the middle of the X. Attach the other end to two more crossed dowels.

Tie the fish onto the dowels, using varying lengths of yarn.

Isaiah's Proclamation Banners

Materials

1 9" × 7" styrofoam meat tray per child	scissors
1 ball of packaging string	pencils and felt-tip pens
several bottles of glue	glue paint (See Recipes and Methods at back of book.)
several small bottles of red or blue paint	
1 foot of heavy rug yarn per child (yarn should be the same color as the glue paint)	

Preparation

Ask a butcher for the number of meat trays you will need. Gather the rest of the materials needed.

Mix the glue paint and put it in small squeeze bottles.

Cut the one-foot lengths of rug yarn.

Make an example to hang on the classroom wall.

Procedure

Give each child a meat tray. Have him use a pencil to lightly write, "The Lord is coming. He shall be called Emmanuel," in the middle of the meat tray. Then use the pencil to make a wavy line around the edge of the meat tray.

Cut a long length of packaging string and glue it along the wavy line. The string may be colored with a felt-tip pen or with a thin layer of glue paint.

Before painting the saying, turn the meat tray over and glue on the ends of the rug yarn to form a hanger.

Turn over the tray and carefully go over each letter in the saying with a thin line of glue paint. Let the glue paint dry thoroughly.

Let the children take the plaques home to hang up.

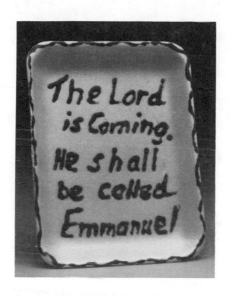

New Testament

1. Birth and Childhood of Jesus

Baby in a Manger

Materials

large and miniature marshmallows scissors

3″ × 3″ squares of flannel yellow yarn

small boxes felt-tip markers

brown construction paper glue

toothpicks

Procedure

Make a manger by covering a small box with brown construction paper. Attach the paper with glue.

Cut yellow yarn into small pieces and lay it in the box to represent hay. Give each child a large and a small marshmallow. Stick a toothpick through the middle of the small marshmallow and then through the larger one. If any one of the toothpicks sticks out, break off the excess. Use felt-tip markers to draw a face on the small marshmallow.

Wrap the square of flannel around the baby and secure the ends with glue. Lay the baby in the manger.

Sandpaper Houses

Materials

sandpaper	scissors
1 sheet of light blue or white construction paper per child	newspaper
	paint shirts
water colors	coloring book with nativity pictures
small brushes	ditto master
glue	ditto paper

Preparation

Find pictures of Joseph, Mary, and Jesus as a child in a coloring book. Trace individual pictures onto a ditto master and duplicate.

Procedure

Color and cut out the pictures of Joseph, Mary, and Jesus.
Cut the sandpaper into small squares.
Lay newspaper on the work area and put on paint shirts.
Give each child a sheet of construction paper. Make a tree trunk for a palm tree by gluing several squares of sandpaper onto the construction

paper. You may want to make more than one tree. Use water colors to paint the top of the tree. Also paint the rest of the background. This may be a mountain or desert scene. Let dry.

Starting at the bottom center of the picture, make a house out of the sandpaper. Fill in most of the house but leave the center blank. Glue the figures in the center of the house.

Water Buffalo Ring Toss Game

Materials

large sturdy paper plates	construction paper
white tagboard	24" dowels
yarn	stapler
pipe cleaners	spray paint

Preparation

Before class spray paint the paper plates. Cut two horn patterns (use the picture for reference). You also may want to make patterns for the eyes, nose, and mouth.

Procedure

Place two plates together and staple around the edges, leaving an opening at the bottom. Insert a dowel into the opening and push it to the top of the plates. Staple around the opening until the dowel is secure.

Cut horns from white tagboard and staple them to the back of the plates.

Cut the facial features from construction paper. Use white for the eyes and glue blue dots on the middle of the eyes. Use pink for the nose. Add small blue dots. Use deep pink for the mouth.

Punch a hole between the horns. Cut two pieces of yarn fifteen inches long. Run one end of each piece of yarn through the hole. Tie securely. On the other end of each piece of yarn tie a pipe cleaner that has been made into a circle.

The object of the game is to flip the pipe cleaner ring up and to catch it on one of the horns.

Carpenter's Tools

Materials

2 8½″ × 11″ sheets of tagboard or heavy construction paper per child
ditto masters
scissors
crayons

Preparation

Before class draw the tools on ditto masters and run them off on sheets of tagboard. (These patterns should be enlarged so that the tools are eight inches long or three to four inches wide.)

Set out the crayons and scissors on the worktable.

Procedure

Give each child a set of tools to color and cut out.

An interesting discussion may be started by asking the children what they feel might be the difference between the tools Joseph used and the tools a carpenter uses today.

Button Whirls

Materials

large, flat button with two holes
yarn

Procedure

String the yarn through the buttonholes and tie the ends. Cut off the excess.

To use, twirl the button on the yarn until the yarn is twisted. Gently and evenly pull the ends to make the button whirl.

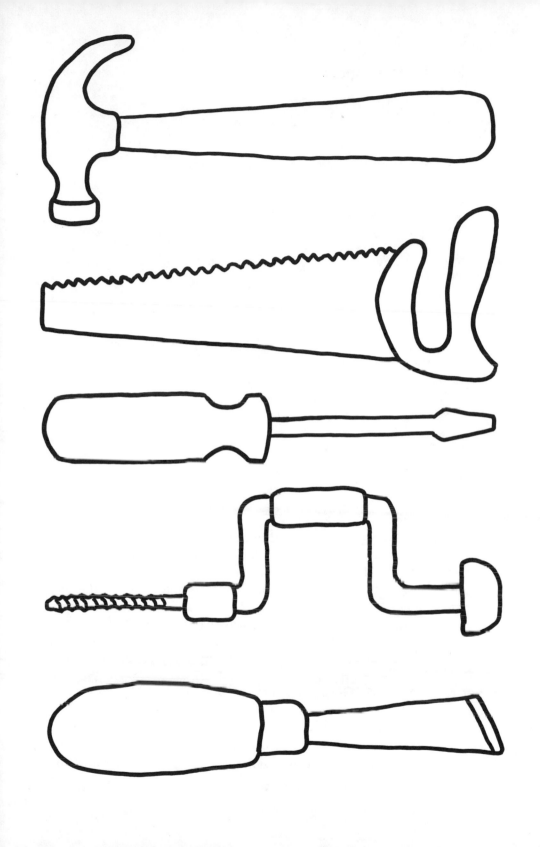

2. John the Baptist

Dove Mobiles

Materials

3 3″ × 5″ sheets of white construction paper per child

3 7″ × 5″ sheets of white construction paper per child

1 small paper bowl per child

blue spray paint

blue yarn

pencils

several nails

rulers

several patterns of doves

needlepoint needles

scissors

blue felt-tip pens

newspapers

Preparation

Cut the sheets of paper to the required sizes. Each child will need three of each size sheet.

Run off patterns of several sizes of doves.

Gather the rest of the materials for the class.

Make a mobile to show as an example.

Procedure

Give each child three sheets of each size of paper. Draw around the dove patterns, placing the larger pattern on the five-by-seven-inch sheets of paper. Cut out the doves.

While the children are working on the doves, spray paint the outside of the bowls. The mobiles will be made with the bowl turned upside down.

Use a felt-tip pen to outline the outside edge of each dove.

Cut three lengths of yarn eight inches long and three lengths of yarn fourteen inches long. Give each child a needle and have him thread a length of yarn into the needle. Tie a knot at the end of the yarn. Thread the yarn through the tail of one of the doves. The hole should be approximately one-half inch from the edge of the tail. Use the long threads with the smaller doves and the shorter threads with the larger doves.

Pass out the bowls and have the children set them upright. The circumference of each bowl should be divided into six equal parts. Mark the divisions near the lip of the bowl. Poke small holes at each of the marked divisions with a nail. Thread the free end of one of the lengths of yarn through a needle. Work up from the bottom of the bowl. Thread the yarn through the hole so that the knot will rest on the top of the lip of the

bowl and the dove will hang down. Tie a knot at the end of each thread after it has been put through a hole. Do this for each of the six doves, alternating the long threads with the shorter ones.

While the children are attaching the doves, cut fifteen-inch lengths of yarn. You will need one per child.

Have each child punch a small hole in the middle of the top of his bowl with a nail. Thread the length of yarn through a needle and knot the end. Thread the yarn from the inside of the bowl up through the top. The knot should be pulled until it rests against the inside of the bowl.

Sand Paintings

Materials

1 5" × 7" sheet of light-colored cardboard per child	brushes
cardboard for supports	glue
several bags of colored sand	paper plates
pencils	scissors
paper cups	newspapers

Preparation

Before class gather the various materials needed. To make supports, cut cardboard triangles with a base four and one-half inches long and six inches high. You will need one support per picture being made.

Fill the paper cups half full with sand. Fill other paper cups with glue. Cover the worktable with newspapers.

Procedure

Give each child a sheet of cardboard and have him draw a pretty picture or design on it. The drawings should be basic. Draw nothing that has fine details. When the pictures are finished, demonstrate to the class how to paint with the sand. Using a brush, evenly cover a small area with glue. Then take a cup of the appropriate colored sand and shake it over the glued area. Pour on enough sand to cover the area well. Pat down the sand and then gently tap the picture over a paper plate to catch the excess sand. Fold the paper plate to make a funnel and pour the excess sand back into the cup. The children should use only one color of sand at a time and work in small areas. When the pictures are finished, they will be entirely covered with sand. Put the pictures aside to dry.

When the pictures are dry, paste the supports onto the back. Give each child a cardboard triangle and have him fold it in half with the right side over the left side. Have the children turn their pictures over and apply glue along the spine of the folded triangle. Center the spine of the triangle on the back of the picture. The base of the triangle should be positioned along the bottom edge of the picture. Hold the triangle until the glue begins to hold. Let dry thoroughly.

Desert Scene

Materials

1 toaster-oven- or microwave-oven-size box	scraps of colored material
1 bag of playground sand	crayons
branches from bushes	aluminum foil
small rocks	scraps of construction paper
dried weeds	yellow clay
atomizer and water	paste
tan or brown chenille pipe cleaners	scissors
	newspapers

Preparation

Cut down the sides of an appliance box, leaving six inches uncut on each side.

Set up the work area outside or in a spot which can be easily cleaned up. Put sand in the box. Moisten the sand so that the children can build up mountains and hills. Have the rest of the materials ready to use except for the items found outside. The children will gather these from the church-yard or a nearby field.

Procedure

Take the class outside to gather branches, small rocks, and anything else that will fit in a desert scene. Bring the various things to the work area.

Divide the class into three groups. One group will work on the desert landscape. Another group will make the figure of John the Baptist and the campfire, and the last group can make the tent and various camp materials.

The group making the landscape will need to make the mountains and hills first. Use rocks to help create a rugged scene. To make a creek the

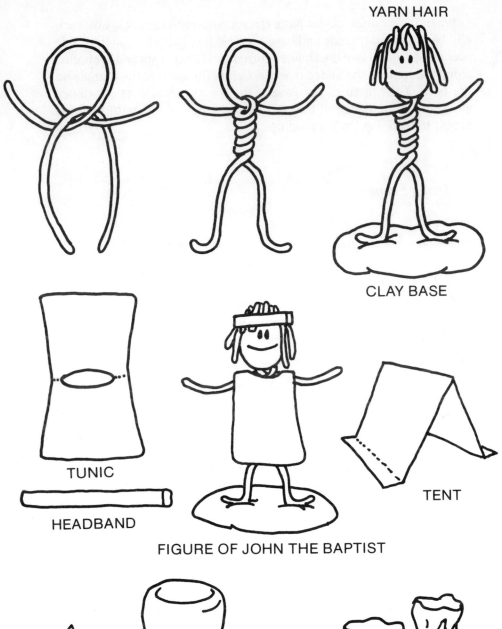

YARN HAIR

CLAY BASE

TUNIC

HEADBAND

FIGURE OF JOHN THE BAPTIST

TENT

FIRE

WATER TANK

COOKING POT

POUCHES

children should make a ditch and line it with foil. Use twigs to form trees, bushes, or a hedge. Use dried weeds for grasses and wild flowers. Fill the creek with water.

To make the figure of John the Baptist, have one child bend the pipe cleaners as shown in the diagram. Have another child cut a circle and draw a face on it. Glue the face to the front of the head. Make hair from brown paper or yarn. One child can cut a small tunic and headband from scrap material.

When the figure has been completed, slip the tunic on the figure and glue the headband around the head. Stick the feet of the figure into a small lump of clay. Set the figure aside until the children are ready to put it in the desert scene.

Stack some twigs to look like a campfire. Make construction paper flames.

The group making the tent should cut a four-by-one-inch rectangle out of brown paper. Fold in half and bend the ends outward.

Water jugs, cooking pots, and pouches may be made from clay.

When all of the groups have finished, arrange the figures in the sand.

Popsicle Stick Frames

Materials

popsicle sticks or craft sticks

glue

small pictures of Jesus being baptized

marker

pop can pull tabs

Procedure

Place the picture on the work surface. Glue one craft stick to each of the four sides, overlapping the ends. Continue to glue the sticks in layers around the picture until you have three layers all the way around.

Glue a pop can pull tab to the back of the frame.

3. Calling of the Disciples

Paraffin Boats

Materials

blocks of paraffin   knife

construction paper   pencil

toothpicks

Procedure

Before you begin carving the boat, use a pencil to mark the areas you want to cut off the wax.

Use a knife to carve the boat.

Cut a small triangle out of construction paper for the sail. Poke holes at the top and bottom of the edge of the sail and weave the toothpick through the holes. Stick the toothpick into the wax.

4. The Miracle Stories

Clay Bowls (Wedding at Cana)

Materials

greenware clay   dinner knives

several rolling pins   several small bowls

thread   pencils

oilcloth or an old sheet   newspapers

7″ × 7″ squares of cardboard

Preparation

Buy a sack of clay from a ceramic store. Make arrangements with the shop to fire the bowls after they have dried. Gather the rest of the materials.

Cover the worktable with newspapers and then place a cloth on top.

Procedure

Give each child a handful of clay and have him knead it until it is soft and pliable. Flatten half of the clay into a rounded mound. Using a rolling pin, roll the clay into a slab about one-half inch thick. Invert a four-to-five-inch bowl over the flattened clay. Cut around the outside of the bowl with a knife. Clear away the scraps of clay and smooth any cracks. Place the clay circle on the square of cardboard and set aside.

Have the children gather the scraps and knead them into the rest of the clay. Add moisture if necessary to keep the clay pliable. Make another slab one-fourth inch thick. Cut strips from the slab two to two and one-half inches wide. These strips will be used to make the sides of the bowl.

Place one strip at a time along the base of the bowl. Attach each strip by smoothing in the cracks between the pieces with a moistened finger. Attach all the strips to the base first, smoothing the joints along the inside and then on the outside of the wall. When the bowl is sturdy take it off the cardboard and smooth the joining cracks along the bottom. Put the bowl back on the cardboard. The top of the bowl may not be perfectly even. To correct it wrap a length of thread around the outside of the bowl. Line up the thread with the lowest point of the top of the bowl. When the ends of the thread are crossed and gently pulled, the thread will cut into the sides of the bowl at the position marked and make an even line across the top of the bowl. Smooth down the top to make a graceful line.

When the bowls are completed have the children use pencils to decorate the sides. Let the bowls dry thoroughly. This takes three to four days. The bowls should be fired in a kiln. Glaze the bowls if you want them to be waterproof. The bowls may be used as planters or knickknacks.

Braille Cards (The Blind Man)

Materials

1 8″ × 10″ index card per child   felt-tip pen
1 medium safety pin per child   ruler

Preparation

Using a felt-tip pen, write, "I am the Way, the Truth, and the Light," on the cards, leaving plenty of space between the letters and having almost an inch of space above each word. Make a Braille letter chart like the one on page 53.

Procedure

Follow the procedure for Braille cards found on page 53.

Thank You Cards (The Healing of the Lepers)

Materials

1 8″ × 10″ sheet of white construction paper per child

4 almost full 4-oz. bottles of glue

red, yellow, blue, and green food coloring

paintbrushes

pencils

1 8″ × 5″ sheet of white typing paper

felt-tip pens

toothpicks

Preparation

Cut the sheets of white construction paper and typing paper to the required sizes.

Open the bottles of glue and add several drops of food coloring. Screw on the tops and shake the bottles until the coloring has mixed throughout the glue.

Procedure

Have each child draw a cheery picture on the front side of a folded sheet of construction paper.

Demonstrate how to use glue paint. It should be squeezed along the outline of the area you desire to color. If you are only outlining, let the glue harden. If you are filling in an area, use a brush to spread the paint. Add more glue paint if necessary. Paint all areas of the same color at one time. To keep the paint from running into the next area let the glue dry before adding the next color. A marbled effect can be created by adding one color to another and using a toothpick to swirl the two colors together. When the picture is finished, set the paper aside until the glue has thoroughly dried.

Give each child a piece of typing paper and have him write, "Thank You for Being You," Love, —— (*child's name*) with felt-tip pens. Glue the typing paper inside the cover of the card.

The cards may be taken home and given to the children's parents.

Spaghetti Fish (Feeding the Five Thousand)

Materials

cooked spaghetti

1 8½″ × 11″ sheet of heavy tagboard per child

glue

Preparation

Cook the spaghetti to a medium texture and put it in a large bowl.
Cut the tagboard into the required size sheets.

Procedure

Give each child a piece of tagboard, some glue, and a small amount of
spaghetti. Put glue on the center of the tagboard. Using one strand of
spaghetti, shape the top half of the fish. Use another strand to shape the
bottom half. Double each of the outside strands and leave the middle
blank or fill in the middle of the fish with more spaghetti.

Bread Banks (Feeding the Five Thousand)

Materials

¼ loaf of frozen bread dough per child	5″ × 3½″ mini loaf pans
paring knives	several sheets of tagboard
embroidery or sharp-pointed scissors	several circle patterns
scissors	polyurethane spray
pencils	newspapers
glue	

Preparation

Buy enough frozen dough bread to make one small loaf per child. Thaw
the frozen bread in the refrigerator overnight. Divide each loaf into
fourths. Place the dough in greased pans. Turn on the oven to warm or
200° and place the bread pans on the top shelf. On the bottom shelf place
a small bowl of water. Let the dough rise in the oven for approximately
one-half hour or until dough has risen to just above the top of the pans.
Bake the bread for one-half hour at 350°. The bread should be golden
brown when done. Take the bread out of the pans and put the loaves in for
fifteen to twenty minutes until the sides and top have become extremely
hard.

Make several one and one-half-inch circle patterns for the children to
use in class. Make an example to show the children.

Procedure

Give each child a loaf of bread and show them how to cut out the
bottom and insides, leaving one-fourth inch along the top and sides. Have
each child scoop out all of the bread until he reaches the hard wall of the

137

loaf. Freeze the scraps of bread until you desire to have the class make bread pudding.

With a paring knife let each child make a slit across the top of the bread wide enough to accept coins easily. On the sheet of tagboard trace around the outside of the bottom of the loaf. Cut out the tagboard.

Trace one of the circular patterns onto the center of the rectangle. Cut around most of the circle, leaving one side intact.

Spray the inside of each bank with polyurethane spray. Let dry. When the spray is dry, have each child glue the tagboard rectangle to the bottom of his bank. Spray the outside of each loaf with polyurethane. Let the spray dry thoroughly.

The children may take their banks home to keep in their rooms. The bread banks also make good mite boxes for saving money for the poor.

5. Sermon on the Mount

Puzzles (Jesus with the Children)

Materials

picture of Jesus with children

ditto master

markers or crayons

clear contact paper

tagboard

scissors

Preparation

Find a good picture of Jesus with children, trace it onto a ditto master, and duplicate it.

Procedure

Color the picture of Jesus and the children. Glue it to a piece of tagboard and cut off any excess. Lay the picture on a piece of clear contact paper and place another piece of clear contact paper face down on the picture. Cut around the edges.

Cut the picture into many shapes and let the children practice putting the puzzle together.

Keep the puzzle in sealed plastic bags.

Macaroni Letter Pendants (Jesus with the Children)

Materials

bright colors of tagboard

glue

macaroni letters

paper punch

yarn or gold cord

Procedure

Cut the tagboard into diamond shapes four inches wide and four inches long. Draw light lines across the center of the diamond to help in correctly placing the letters. Carefully glue on one macaroni letter at a time to write, "Jesus Loves Me, This I Know."

Use a paper punch to make a hole at the top of each pendant and string yarn or cord through the hole, making sure that the yarn is long enough to slip over the head. Tie the ends.

You may want to use cord to outline the edges of the diamond.

"Come as a Child" Poster (Jesus with the Children)

Materials

large sheet of fluorescent colored tagboard

scissors

old magazines

glue

picture of Jesus

Preparation

Across the top of the tagboard write in large bold lettering, "Come as a Child."

Procedure

Glue the picture of Jesus in the middle of the tagboard.

Look through magazines to find pictures of children of all nations, religions, and races. Glue the pictures of the children around the picture of Jesus.

Hang up to display.

"I Thank God" Banners

Materials

magazines	scissors
1 12″ × 15″ sheet of light-colored con-struction paper per child	paste or rubber cement
	pencil
various colors of medium-weight yarn	stapler
glue	

Preparation

Gather the required materials. In the center of each sheet of paper, write, "I Thank God," "It Is Good," or any other appropriate saying in large block letters.

Make a banner to show the children.

Procedure

Have the children go through the magazines and find four or five pictures which represent things that they like. These may be pictures of a baby, a pet, a favorite toy, or food. The pictures should not be too large. When the children are finished cutting out the pictures, give them all sheets of construction paper and have them arrange and paste the pictures around the verse in a pleasant manner.

Put several colors of yarn on the table. The children should measure and cut the length of yarn needed to cover each of the letters in the verse. Glue the yarn on top of the letters. Set aside to dry.

Before taking the banners home, have each child cut a two-foot length of yarn and staple one of the ends to each side of the top of the banner to make a hanger.

6. Prayer

Prayer Poster

Materials
1 large light-colored poster board
colored felt-tip pens
1 blue or red felt-tip marker
scrap paper
pencils

Preparation
In the center of the board write, "Our Prayers," with a marker.

Procedure
Pass out the scrap paper and pencils. Tell the children that the class is going to make a prayer poster. Have each child write his prayer on scrap paper.

When the prayers have been completed, lay the poster on the floor and have each child choose a colored pen and find a place to write his prayer.

When finished, hang up the poster in a prominent place to remind the children of the importance of prayer.

7. The Parables

Geometric Designs from Circles (The Lost Coin)

Materials

1 10″ × 10″ sheet of dark-colored construction paper per child

1 compass per child

several boxes of colored chalk

pencils

fixative spray

scrap paper

Preparation

Gather the materials needed for the lesson. Make a few examples to show the children what they can do with their designs.

Procedure

Give each child a compass, a pencil, and some scrap paper. Demonstrate how to use a compass. Let the children practice on scrap paper. Give each a sheet of dark-colored paper. Make one large circle in the middle of the paper. Then draw smaller circles around the larger one. Draw as many circles as desired. The more circles, the more intricate the design will be.

Show the children what can be done by coloring with chalk. Have the children color the different sections of their design with colored chalk. The more variety the children use, the prettier their designs will be.

Spray each of the designs with a fixative spray. Let the spray dry.

Use the pictures to make a colorful bulletin board.

Mustard Seed Necklaces

Materials

1″ × 1″ pieces of wood

white paint

gold glitter

gold ribbon or cord

brush

glue

sandpaper

small eye screw

mustard seeds

newspaper

Procedure

Lay newspaper on the work surface.

Sand the edges of the wood until they are smooth. Paint the wood with white tempera paint or gold spray paint. Let dry. Put a hole in the top center of the block with an eye screw.

142

Cover one side of the wood with glue and sprinkle gold glitter on it. Shake off the excess onto newspaper.

Glue a mustard seed to the middle of the front side of the wood. Run a piece of ribbon or cord through the hole and tie the ends. Make sure the ribbon will fit over a child's head.

Peach Pit Flower Plaques (The Sower)

Materials

1 7″ × 5″ piece of plywood per child	paper towels
beige spray paint	small bag of dried green peas
peach, plum, nectarine, or apricot pits	glue
macaroni	permanent markers
green food coloring	clear shellac or spray varnish
small plastic bags	construction paper

Preparation

Cut the wood into seven-by-five-inch pieces. Paint with beige paint and let dry. Shellac or varnish and let dry.

Put the macaroni into a plastic bag with a few drops of food coloring. Shake the bag until the macaroni is dyed but not wet. Place on paper towels and let dry.

Procedure

Run a thin line of glue on the underside of a split peach pit (or whatever kind of pit you are using). Glue securely to the wood. This will be the center of the flower. You may glue on several split pits for the center. You may also wish to use pits for the petals of the flowers. If you use pits only as centers, you will want to cut petals from construction paper and glue these on the wood first and then cover the ends with the pit.

Use the green macaroni for stems and leaves. Split green peas also make good leaves.

8. Jesus and the Moneychangers

Leather Drawstring Purses

Materials
vinyl, fake fur, or leather
leather shoestrings
paper punch

Procedure
Cut the vinyl, fake fur, or leather into two ten-inch circles per child. Punch holes around the circumference about one inch apart and one inch in from the edge.

Weave the leather shoestring through the holes, leaving about six inches on each end. Gather the strings together to make a drawstring purse. Tie a knot at the end of each string.

9. Passover

Prayer Pretzels

Materials

1 c. warm water	coarse salt
2 packages dry yeast	large bowl
2 tbs. sugar	spoon
3 c. flour	knife
2 tsp. baking soda	shallow pan
butter or margarine	cookie sheet
1 egg	

Long ago in Europe a monk gave children "crossed arms" for learning their prayers. These became what we call pretzels.

Preparation
Put the warm water into a large bowl and add the yeast. Stir until the yeast dissolves. Gradually add the flour and sugar. The mixture will

144

become stiff. Sprinkle some flour on the table and knead the dough until it is smooth. Form the dough into a ball, put it back into the bowl, and cover it with a towel. Let it rise in a warm place for about an hour.

Procedure

Punch down the dough. On the floured table roll the dough into a square about one-half inch thick. Use the dull side of a knife to cut strips about one-fourth inch wide. Twist each strip into a pretzel.

Place the pretzels one at a time in a shallow pan coated with baking soda. Remove each pretzel after five seconds and place it on a buttered cookie sheet. Brush with the beaten egg and sprinkle with salt. Bake in a hot oven (400°) for twelve to fifteen minutes or until golden brown.

10. The Fruit of the Spirit

Chain of Love

Materials
construction paper
markers
glue
small picture of Jesus

Preparation

Cut several construction paper strips two inches wide and six inches long.

Procedure

On each strip draw a small picture of a person you love. Write the name of the person under the picture. Glue a small picture of Jesus on one strip. Use three more strips to write, "I Love You," (one word per strip).

To make the chain, start with the "I Love You" chains and the picture of Jesus. Attach these together by putting a small dab of glue on both ends of the first strip. Glue together. Loop the second strip through the first strip and glue the ends. Continue in the same manner so that when finished you have "I Love You" and the picture of Jesus in the middle and the other pictures on either side.

Paper Dot Picture of Prodigal Son (Love)

Materials

1 12″ × 10″ sheet of light-colored construction paper per child

1 ditto master

coloring book picture of a scene from
the prodigal son parable

1 bowl of black, brown, blue, red, flesh,
and green paper dots

several paper punches or a three-hole
punch

small cups of glue

brushes

Preparation

Find a picture of a scene from the prodigal son parable. Ditto the picture on construction paper. Make an example for the children.

Procedure

Give each child a picture and show him how to spread glue in a small area with a brush. He should quickly lay the dots on the glued area. A small amount of space should be left between the dots. Have the child cover the entire picture, using the appropriate colored dots to fill in the face, hair, clothes, etc.

When finished, display the children's pictures on a bulletin board.

Good Deed Booklets (Kindness)

Materials

sample pieces of wallpaper

construction paper

markers

glue

stapler

paper punch

yarn

Preparation

Cut the wallpaper and the construction paper into four-by-six-inch rectangles.

Procedure

On one side of the construction paper put a small amount of glue in each corner. Glue the paper to the back of the wallpaper. Lay three more pieces of paper on top of the construction paper. Fold all the sheets inside the wallpaper and secure by stapling along the left edge of the front.

Punch a hole in the top and the bottom, leaving a margin. Run the yarn through the holes and tie with a bow in the front. On the front in bold letters write, "My Good Deed Booklet."

Explain to the children that they are to write their own books by recording the good deeds that they do for their neighbors, family, and God.

Good Deed Booklets (Kindness)

Materials

1 20" × 5" sheet of light-colored construction paper for every four children in the class

1 wallet picture of each child in the class

colored felt-tip pens

pictures of people helping others

paste

scissors

Preparation

Send a note home the week before starting this lesson, asking that each child bring a small school picture of himself.

Cut the sheets of paper to the required size.

Procedure

Divide the class into groups of four. Have the children fold the paper into fifths like an accordion. The paper should be turned so that the cover will open as a book would. The outside page is the cover. Each of the inside pages will be for one of the children in the group. Have each child paste his picture on the top part of the page and write his name below it.

Cut out a picture of someone helping another and paste it to the front cover. The children should write, "Our Good Deed Booklet," in block letters around the picture.

The purpose of the booklets is to encourage the children to help others. Each week for three weeks have the children write down the good deeds that they have done throughout the week. These should be written under the child's name.

For competition, offer a special treat or award to the group who does the most good deeds.

Butterfly Bracelets (Gentleness)

Materials

5" cardboard tubes (These can come from a large roll of wrapping paper, copying machine paper, or newsprint.)

sturdy cutting knife

self-drying clay or glue dough

food coloring or pastel shades of acrylic paint

newspapers

dull knives

spatulas

oilcloth

small brushes

clear acrylic paint

bowls of water

Preparation

Gather the materials listed above.

See the recipe for glue dough under Recipes and Methods at the back of the book. Food coloring may be added to the water, eliminating the need for acrylic paint. Mix one or two batches of white dough. A smaller amount of pink, yellow, green, and orange dough will be needed for the butterflies. Put the dough in plastic bags to keep it moist.

Cut the large rolls of cardboard tubing into one-inch widths (one or two per child).

Cover the worktable with oilcloth.

Procedure

Give each child a cardboard ring and have him cover it with a thin layer of dough or clay. Smooth cracks together with a moistened finger. It is all right if the dough has a bumpy appearance.

Use a small amount of colored dough to make several small butterflies and flowers. The dough should be flattened with the palm of the hand and then cut into the desired shapes. Decorate the butterflies and flowers with other colors of dough. Make enough to cover the top of each bracelet. Lift the pieces with a spatula. Attach each of the butterflies and flowers by moistening the clay underneath them. Let the bracelets dry thoroughly.

The next week paint the bracelets if necessary. When finished, spray them with a thin coat of clear acrylic to seal the pores of the clay or dough.

The girls can keep the bracelets. The boys may want to give their bracelets to a sister, cousin, friend, or to their mothers.

148

Silhouettes (Patience)

Materials

black construction paper

white construction paper

scissors

black markers

lamp

large sheet of white butcher paper

Preparation

Hang a large sheet of white butcher paper on the wall. Place a lamp a short distance from the paper. Set a chair between the lamp and the paper.

Procedure

Set one of the children in the chair so that the light casts a profile shadow onto the butcher paper. Make sure the child sits very still. Draw around the outline of the shadow. Cut that section of the paper off the large sheet and rehang the remainder.

Let the child cut around the outline that you drew. Lay the outline on black construction paper and trace around it. Carefully cut it out and mount it with the glue on the white construction paper. On the top of the picture leave enough room to write, "Please be patient with me—God isn't finished with me yet."

11. The Gifts of the Spirit

Necklaces for Teachers

Materials

modeling compound

cookie sheets

spatulas

water-based acrylic paints

paper clips

dull knives

oilcloth

medium-weight yarn

utensils for modeling clay

small paintbrushes

small bowls of water

Preparation

Buy a box of modeling compound. Gather the rest of the materials. Make a few examples.

Cover the worktable with oilcloth. Set several bowls of water on the table.

Procedure

Have the children think about what they would like to put on a pendant for one of their teachers at school. They could decorate the pendants with flowers, butterflies, birds, or with the school mascot.

Give each child a handful of modeling compound and have him knead it until it is soft and pliable. Roll some of the clay out to make a base. To avoid having the compound stick to the work area, dampen the oilcloth surface and the rolling pin. The base should be approximately one-fourth to one-half inch thick. The size of the base will depend on how large the child wants to make the pendant. On the backside press in a paper clip to make a hook.

To make the decorative pieces, roll each section one-fourth inch thick. Cut out a flower, butterfly, or whatever is being used for decoration. To make two pieces stick together, moisten them.

When finished, lift the pendants onto a cookie sheet and bake the pieces at 325° for approximately fifteen minutes. The clay will be hard when finished. Let the figures cool.

Paint the figures with appropriate colors. When dry, cut a length of yarn fifteen inches long and thread it through the paper clip. Tie the ends.

Memory Books (Knowledge)

Materials

2 5″ circles cut from light-colored construction paper per child	scissors
	ditto master
10 5″ circles cut from white typing paper per child	pencils
	transparent tape
several fine-point, felt-tip pens	paste
brads	paper punch
small pictures of the apostles	

Preparation

Cut out the circles from the appropriate paper.

Buy three-by-two-inch pictures of the apostles from a religious book-

150

store. Make a chart of ten of Jesus' sayings (your choice) for the children to copy.

Gather the rest of the materials.

Make an example to show the children.

Procedure

Give each child ten white circles and have him copy one saying on each.

When finished, round the edges of a picture of the apostles. Paste the picture in the center of the construction paper circle to make the booklet cover. Using a felt-tip pen, write, "And They Taught the Teachings of Jesus," around the picture.

To assemble the booklets, put the construction paper covers on each side of the filler pages. Punch a hole on the left side of the booklet. Push the brad through the hole and spread the tabs. Anchor the tabs with tape.

Have the children use these for memory booklets.

Gifts of the Spirit Books

Materials

9 empty matchbooks per child

construction paper

felt-tip markers

glue

scissors

Preparation

Empty the matchbooks. Cut several pieces of construction paper the same width and length as the matchbooks.

Procedure

Cover the outside of each matchbook with glue. Place it on a piece of construction paper. With a marker write the name of one gift of the Spirit on the spine and on the cover. You also may want to cover the inside with construction paper. Follow this procedure for each of the nine gifts.

You may want to make a bookcase by covering a small box with construction paper.

This craft makes it easy for the children to learn the gifts of the Spirit.

Cards for the Ill (Healing)

Materials

1 warming tray (used for keeping dishes hot during buffets)

1 sheet of foil to cover the warming tray

1 10″ × 5″ sheet of white construction paper per child

crayons with wrapping removed

1 10″ × 5″ sheet of white typing paper per child

felt-tip pens

paste

cloth

hot pad

Preparation

Obtain a warming tray and cover it with foil. The foil should be wrapped securely so that it will not come off while being used.

Cut the sheets of construction paper and typing paper to the correct size.

Locate several short poems or salutatory greetings for the children to use. If possible, obtain a list of ill people in the church or the names of those residing in a nearby nursing home. It will seem more personal if the cards are addressed to specific people.

Procedure

Demonstrate how to print with the melted crayon. Heat the tray to the temperature needed to melt crayons. Make a swirling design on the foil, using several colors of crayon. When finished, immediately lay a piece of construction paper on top of the design and rub the paper with your hand, protected by a hot pad. Lift off the paper. The melted crayon design will have been transferred to it. Put the paper aside to dry. Wipe off the excess crayon.

While the crayon on the outside of the cards is drying, have the children copy the poem or salutatory greeting which they feel is appropriate for their card. They should put the verse on the right half of the sheet of typing paper. When finished, have them sign their name and the church they represent. The sheets of typing paper should be pasted inside of the printed cards. If you have time, let the children make envelopes for the cards.

Take the cards to the people for whom they were made. The recipients will find great pleasure in being remembered. The experience teaches the children that it is nice to do things for others.

12. Communities

Three-dimensional Maps

Materials

world map
old magazines
glue
scissors
straight pins

Procedure

Hang a world map on the wall low enough for the children to reach.

Have the children cut out pictures of people from around the world. (National Geographic is an excellent magazine for this craft.) As the children cut out the pictures, glue or pin the pictures onto the areas of the map where those people live.

Seasonal Crafts

1. Autumn

Leaf Pictures

Materials

leaves

2 8″ × 10″ pieces of clear contact paper per child

small bags

Procedure

Give the children bags and take them outdoors to gather leaves.

Cut eight-by-ten-inch pieces of clear contact paper and peel off the backing.

Have the children arrange the leaves on the sticky side of the contact paper, leaving at least one-inch clear on all sides.

Peel off the backing on second pieces of contact paper and carefully place them over the leaves. The children will need help, so do this step individually.

Hot Plates

Materials

6″ squares of scrap lumber about 1″ thick

small individual ceramic tiles

small pictures or decals of autumn leaves

glue

wrapping paper

Preparation

Cut, sand, and stain the wood pieces.

Procedure

Give each child a piece of wood and a few tiles. Let the child glue the tile to form a pattern on the wood.

Paste pictures or decals of autumn leaves on the tiles.

Wrap the hot plate and have the child present it as a gift to his mother.

Spice Wreaths

Materials

small styrofoam rings	glue
spices	red ribbon
green florist tape	scissors
cloves	straight pins

Preparation

Make a wreath as an example.

Procedure

Wrap the styrofoam ring with green florist tape. Overlap each turn to make the tape lie flat. Glue the end to secure and cut off the excess tape.

Poke whole cloves close together all the way around the outside and inside edges of the ring.

Put a small amount of glue on one area of the front of the ring. Choose one of the spices and sprinkle it onto the glue. Shake off the excess and continue in the same manner with other spices until the entire front of the wreath is covered. With a piece of red ribbon make a bow and attach it to the front of the top of the wreath with a straight pin.

2. Halloween

Pumpkin Seed Pictures

Materials

dried pumpkin seeds

1 large sheet of dark-colored
construction paper per child

pencils

glue

Preparation

Gather the pumpkin seeds from several pumpkins. Have the rest of the materials ready.

Make an example to show the children.

Procedure

Give each child a sheet of paper and a pencil and have him draw a very simple Halloween scene. Point out that they will need only a basic outline for the figures in the picture.

When the children are finished drawing, have them outline the figures with seeds. Glue the seeds on the paper to make a picket fence, the silhouette of a haunted house, or an eerie tree. Let the glue dry thoroughly.

Hang up the pictures on a bulletin board.

Cats

Materials

1 12" × 8" sheet of black construction
paper per child

1 6" × 6" sheet of black construction
paper per child

several sheets of tagboard for patterns

1 ditto master of a large cat

scraps of white and red construction
paper

scissors

paste

pencils

Preparation

Run off several patterns of the cat's body as shown below. The patterns should be approximately twelve by eight inches. Cut the smaller squares of black paper.

Gather the rest of the materials.

Make an example to show the children.

Procedure

On the large sheet of black paper have each child trace around the cat pattern. Cut the pattern from the large sheet. On the square of black paper draw a spiral line starting from the outside edge and ending in the center. Cut along the line and cut off the outside edge. The spiral is the cat's tail. Paste the tail onto the cat.

Using scraps of paper, cut out the eyes, nose, whiskers, mouth, and a bow. Paste these on the cat.

Have the child hold his cat to see how the tail wiggles.

Crayon Relief Pictures

Materials

1 large sheet of light-colored construction paper per child	newspapers
	paint shirts
crayons	black India ink
several small bowls	several brushes

Preparation

Gather the required materials. Make an example to show the children.

Set up a painting table and a drying area. Each should be covered with newspapers.

Procedure

Have the children think of what they might find on a scary Halloween night. They might think of a haunted house, black cats, ghosts, or witches. Have the children use crayons to draw a scary Halloween night scene. They should use light colors and color heavily. The wax of the crayon must cover the paper or the ink will soak through it.

Put on paint shirts. Instruct the children to cover their papers with black India ink. When the children spread the ink over their pictures, they will see that it beads up on the crayon wax and the color shows through to create an eerie effect. Set the papers aside to dry.

3. Thanksgiving

Turkey Centerpieces

Materials

1 large apple per child	raisins
cranberries	large marshmallows
toothpicks	black felt-tip pens
1 6″ × 6″ sheet of yellow or light green construction paper per child	scissors

Preparation

Put the raisins, cranberries, marshmallows, and toothpicks in small bowls. Make a sample turkey for the children to use as a guide.

Procedure

Give each child a large apple. Push a toothpick into the apple to make the neck of the turkey. Push four or five raisins onto the toothpick. Use a marshmallow to make the head. Cut away part of the marshmallow to form a beak. Slide the marshmallow onto the end of the toothpick. Use a black felt-tip pen to make an eye on each side of the head.

To make the tail feathers for the turkey, stick five or six toothpicks into the apple. Put raisins on the first toothpick and cranberries on the next. Alternate until all the toothpicks are full.

Cut a wavy line all around the edges of the construction paper to make a base for the centerpiece. Make small cuts into the paper all the way around the edges and then curl the edges with a pencil to look like grass.

Turkeys

Materials

large pinecones	construction paper
small styrofoam balls	glue
pipe cleaners	brown paint and brushes

Procedure

Paint the small styrofoam ball with brown paint and let dry. This is the turkey's head.

Poke a pipe cleaner about one-half inch into the ball. Wrap the other end around one end of a pinecone and bend the middle to form the neck. The pinecone is the body. Stick two short pieces of pipe cleaner into the bottom for feet. From construction paper cut a small eye and a beak and glue them to the head.

Using several colors of paper, cut out narrow ovals about four inches long. On each of these strips have the children print the name of something for which they are thankful. Glue each of the strips into the end of the pinecone to form the tail.

4. Advent—Christmas

Tissue Paper Wreaths

Materials

green tissue paper

scissors

coat hangers

red ribbon

Preparation

Cut the tissue paper into small strips approximately five inches long. Bend the coat hangers so that they form a circle. Leave the hooks attached to use as hangers for the wreaths.

Procedure

Starting at the middle of the coat hanger, wrap one piece of tissue paper around the hanger, twist, and tie. Continue up one side, placing each piece very close to the next. When one side is finished, do the other side in the same manner until the coat hanger is completely covered. Pull on the ends gently to fluff up the paper. Make a bow from red ribbon and tie it at the top of the wreath.

Popcorn Christmas Trees

Materials

styrofoam tree shapes
straight pins
popped popcorn
small glass balls
thin red and green ribbon

Preparation

Pop the popcorn.
Lay newspaper on the work area.

Procedure

Stick a straight pin through one kernel of corn and then into the styrofoam tree. Continue in this manner until the tree is completely covered. Make sure that you place the popcorn close together.
Make several small bows out of ribbon and stick them on the tree.
Put a small dot of glue on each glass ball and glue it to the tree.

Napkin Holders

Materials

1 cardboard roll from toilet tissue per child
2 2½" × 5¾" pieces of red and green felt per child
2 18" lengths of red or green rickrack or gold cording per child
glue
scissors

Preparation

Cut the cardboard tubes in half. Cut the rickrack and the felt into the necessary lengths.

Procedure

Apply thin lines of glue along the bottom and top of the cardboard tube. Center the felt on the tube and fold the edges under. Apply glue around the inside edges of the tube to secure the ends of the felt. Cover each of the rolls.

Tie rickrack around the center of the roll. Tie a knot and then make a bow. Apply a small drop of glue underneath the bow to secure the rickrack to the felt.

Pinecone Centerpieces

Materials

styrofoam cones	small tin can (not over 2″ high)
small pinecones	brown burlap
glue	straight pins
thin green ribbon	

Preparation

Cut the burlap to fit around the tin cans.

Procedure

Put a small amount of glue on a pinecone and attach it to the styrofoam cone. Start at the bottom and continue attaching the pinecones until the styrofoam cone is covered. Let dry.

Glue the burlap onto the tin can. Glue the pinecone tree to the top of the can. Let dry.

Tie several small bows and attach them with straight pins to the pinecones.

Stained Glass Murals

Materials

large sheets of white butcher paper	newspaper
salad oil	permanent black markers
crayons	paint shirts
paper towels	

Preparation

Draw simple pictures on the large sheets of butcher paper. You may want to make the pictures in a sequence to tell a story. Use as few details as possible.

Lay newspaper on the work area.

Tape the drawings down with masking tape. Use a thick marker to draw black lines around the edges to make a stained glass effect.

Procedure

Put paint shirts on all the children. Pour a little oil on each picture and spread it out to the edges with paper towel.

Have the children color in all areas of the mural with crayons. They will have to color heavily. To make the picture brighter, turn over and color the other side. Let dry.

Hang the picture in a window.

Advent Wreath

This lesson should be done before Advent.

Materials *(For each wreath being made)*

2 1' boards ½" thick and 1" wide	3 purple, 1 rose, and 1 white candle
5 large screw-on bottle caps	hammer
florist clay	pliers
2 short nails	green spray paint
glue	newspapers
fresh pine greens	

Preparation

Cut the boards before class. Glue and nail the boards together to form the base crosses.

Make an example for use in the classroom.

Procedure

Glue on the bottle caps, putting one at the end of each stick and one in the center. Let the glue dry. Spray paint the boards with green spray paint.

Lay the cross in the center of a table and cover with fresh pine greens. Put three purple candles in the end holders. Put the rose candle in the remaining end holder. Put the white candle in the center. If the candles are wobbly, put some florist clay in the bottom of each candleholder to help secure the candles.

5. Winter

Birdseed Cookies

Materials

bread	peanut butter
birdseed	cornmeal
red yarn	large metal cookie cutters
knives	scissors
2-3 large nails	

Preparation

Several days before making the birdseed cookies, lay out the bread so that it will become hard.

Make a mixture of three parts peanut butter and one part cornmeal.

Make a cookie for an example.

Procedure

Cut a slice of bread with a cookie cutter. Make a hole in the top of the bread with a nail. Thread a length of yarn approximately one-foot long though the hole and tie the ends together. Spread the top of the bread cookie with the peanut butter mixture. Sprinkle with birdseed.

Hang the cookies in a tree that the children can see from inside the classroom.

Snowflakes

Materials

9″ × 9″ squares of white paper	heavy scissors
dark construction paper	straight pins

Preparation

Draw an eight-inch circle on each of the sheets of white paper.

Cover a bulletin board with dark construction paper.

Procedure

Cut out the circle and fold it in half. Then fold the semicircle in half. Cut out designs from the two folded sides. Scallop the outside edge and cut off the very tip of the cone. Be sure to leave some of the paper along the folds intact so that the snowflake will hold together. Carefully unfold the snowflake.

Pin the children's snowflakes onto the bulletin board. The dark paper will make the snowflakes stand out.

Frosting-painted Winter Scenes

Materials

1 recipe of frosting paint	glue
popsicle sticks	small bowls
1 9″ × 12″ sheet of blue construction paper per child	scraps of construction paper
	scissors
1 9″ × 12″ sheet of cardboard or tag-board	

Preparation

Mix one recipe of frosting paint. (See Recipes and Methods at back of book for instructions.)

Gather the rest of the materials.

Procedure

Give each child a sheet of blue construction paper and cardboard. Glue the construction paper onto the cardboard.

Using popsicle sticks, have the children paint winter scenes on the paper. The white frosting can be used for snowpeople and snow. Pine trees, water, hats, shawls, faces, and so forth can be fashioned out of the scraps of construction paper. When finished, lay the pictures aside to dry. It will take a couple of days for the frosting to dry thoroughly.

6. St. Valentine's Day

Valentine People

Materials

1 6" × 10" sheet of light blue construction paper per child

1 3" square of red construction paper per child

1 2" square of red construction paper per child

4 1" squares of red construction paper per child

5 3" × ½" strips of white construction paper per child

scraps of colored construction paper

brown, yellow, and black yarn

doilies

scissors

blue felt-tip pen

crepe paper

tissue paper

pencils

paste

Preparation

Cut paper into the required sizes.

Make an example of a valentine person.

Procedure

Give each child one three-inch square, one two-inch square, and four one-inch squares. Review how to make a heart by folding a square in half and drawing half of a heart on the fold. Cut out and unfold. This procedure should be used to make the hearts for the body, head, hands, and feet.

When ready to assemble the body, have each child paste the ends of the four white strips on the back of the largest valentine heart in the positions where the arms and legs would naturally be. Also, have the children cut a three-inch strip in half for the neck. Paste it in place. Turn the body over and paste one of the four smaller hearts at the end of each of the arms and legs. The medium-sized heart should be pasted on the short neck strip to form the head. Use pieces of scrap paper and yarn to make facial features and hair.

Paste the valentine person onto the sheet of light blue paper. Use pieces of scrap paper, doilies, yarn, crepe or tissue paper to make the clothes for the person.

When finished, have each child write the name of his person in an arch across the top of the background sheet.

The valentine people make excellent decorations for a bulletin board.

Valentine Cards

Materials

medium-sized white doilies	glue
1 6" × 6" piece of red construction paper per child	scissors
	fine-tip marker
small pictures of Jesus	

Preparation

Cut the red construction paper to the appropriate size. Make a card to use as an example.

Procedure

Have each child draw a heart on a folded piece of red construction paper and cut it from the paper. Make sure that the child does not cut the fold. Put a small amount of glue on the backside of the folded heart and attach it to the center of a doily. The fold should be on the left. Open the heart and glue the small picture of Jesus on the right side of the inside of the heart. On the front of the heart, write, "I Love You."

Peek Cards

Materials

red construction paper	glue
small picture of Jesus	marker
scissors	X-Acto knife

Procedure

Cut out a few hearts about seven inches tall to use as patterns.

Have each child trace two hearts onto red construction paper and cut them out. In the center of one of the hearts glue a picture of Jesus and run a thin line of glue around the outside edge. Glue the other heart on top of it. Use a pencil to carefully mark by feeling where the picture is centered between the two hearts. An adult should carefully use an X-Acto knife to cut around three sides of the picture. Fold back the fourth side to expose the picture. On the front heart write, "Jesus Loves Me."

7. St. Patrick's Day

Pig Crayon Holder

Materials

1 gallon-size bleach or milk bottle per child

4 small corks per child

1 yd. each of several different colors of contact paper or several sheets of brightly colored construction paper

1 sheet each of black and white construction paper per child

lace

chenille pipe cleaners (the color should be coordinated with the color of the lace)

scissors

glue and transparent tape

Preparation

The week before you intend to do this lesson, send a note home with each child, asking that he bring a gallon-size bleach or milk bottle from home. Have a few extra bottles on hand.

Cut out several circle and eye patterns.

Make an example.

Procedure

On the side of the bottle opposite the side with the handle cut four holes. Two holes should go on either end. Corks will be inserted into these holes as feet. Have an adult cut out a large rectangle from the top of the pig's body.

Have each child use the circle patterns to cut ten circles from the colored paper. He should also cut out two white and two black eye circles.

Glue the eye circles in place on both sides of the handle at the back of the depression where the handle starts. Glue the other circles around the body in a polka dot design or in clusters of two or three.

While the children are gluing the circles in place, measure the amount of lace needed to go around the spout. Cut a length of lace for each child. Each child will glue the lace in place, holding it until it begins to adhere.

Give each child a pipe cleaner and have him twist the end around a pencil to make a curly tail. Glue or tape the tail onto the rear of the bottle.

Spread glue around the top end of each of the corks and stick them into the holes cut in the bottom of the bottle. This will help to secure the feet. Let the glue dry before the pigs are picked up.

Read the story of St. Patrick. Note that when he first arrived on the British Isles there was very little to eat so he hunted wild pigs to keep from starving.

Have the children take the pigs home and use them to keep their crayons, colored pencils, and felt-tip pens in order.

8. Easter

Cross Cards

Materials

doilies

glue

yellow construction paper

felt-tip markers

wallet-size pictures of Jesus

Procedure

Cut out several crosses eight inches long by four and one-half inches wide to use for patterns. Give each child one of the patterns and a sheet of yellow construction paper. Fold the paper in half lengthwise. Place the pattern on the fold so that one arm of the cross touches the fold. Trace around the cross and cut it from the paper, being careful not to cut the folded edge.

Open up the cross. In the center of the inside glue a small picture of Jesus.

Glue the cross in the center of a doily. On the front print across the crossbeam, "He Is Risen."

Eggshell Mosaic Crosses

Materials

1 or 2 large sheets of white or tan poster board

eggshells

blue food coloring

vinegar

dark blue fine-tip, felt-tip pens

pencils

scissors

rolling pins

glue

plastic bags

rulers

blue yarn

pop can pull tabs

paper towels

Preparation

Cut the poster board into ten-by-fifteen-inch rectangles (one per child). Dye a dozen eggshells blue and then peel them for the class or have each child bring in eggshells and dye them.

Gather the rest of the materials.

Make an example to show the children.

Procedure

If the eggshells have not been dyed, put them in a bowl with several drops of blue food coloring and one to two tablespoons of vinegar. Add enough water to cover the eggshells. Leave them in the bowl for a few minutes and then take them out and dry them on a paper towel.

Pass out a sheet of poster board, a ruler, and a pencil to each child. Have him draw a cross twelve by eight inches wide in the center of the board. Set aside when finished.

Put the dried eggshells in a plastic bag and crush them with a rolling pin. Spread a thin layer of glue on the inside of each cross. Sprinkle the eggshells on top of the wet glue. Turn over any pieces of white eggshell. Pat the shells to make sure they adhere to the paper.

Give each child a length of blue yarn. Paint a thin line of glue around the outside edge of the cross. Lay the yarn on top of the glue.

In the lower right corner of the poster board write, "Christ Died to Save Us," in a diagonal line.

On the back of the poster board, glue a pop can pull tab to the center of the top edge. This will serve as a picture hanger.

Have the children take the boards home and hang them in a prominent place.

9. Spring

Pansy Bookmarks

Materials

metal hair clips

various colors of tissue paper

glue

thin wire

pencils

scissors

Procedure

Cut the tissue paper into strips two inches long and one inch wide. Curl the strip of tissue paper around the middle of a pencil and hold. Slip out the pencil carefully and the tissue paper will stay curled. Do this with several colors.

Cut small circles from yellow tissue paper or use a paper punch to punch out the circles.

Gather the strips of tissue paper together. Put a small dab of glue on the end of each of the strips and attach one to another, forming a flower. Glue the yellow dot in the center where the ends meet. Gently push both ends of a folded piece of wire through the center. The ends will now be on the backside of the flower. Slip both ends through the top of a hair clip. Twist the wires to secure and cut off the excess.

To use the bookmark, open the clip and attach it to the page you wish to mark.

10. Gifts

Verse Plaques

Materials

1 12″ × 10″ board per child

medium-colored wood stain

1 sheet of white typing paper per child

red, yellow, orange, and green construction paper

flower and leaf patterns

scissors

black felt-tip pen

poem appropriate for the occasion

clear acrylic spray paint

picture hangers

pencils

rubber cement

tissue paper

glue

Preparation

Cut out, sand, and stain the wood plaque.

Prepare the flower and leaf patterns. The flowers can be tulips, daisies, pansies or any other simple flower.

Cut out eight-by-ten-inch ovals from typing paper. Write the verse or poem on each with a permanent ink felt-tip pen. The waterproof ink will not run when the acrylic paint is sprayed on the finished plaque. Glue a picture hanger on the back of each plaque with a couple drops of super glue.

Procedure

Have the children cut out several flowers and leaves from different colors of construction paper. Make enough flowers to surround the outside of the verse.

When the flowers are finished, have each child glue the verse onto the center of the board. Glue on the flowers and leaves in a pleasant manner, covering the outside edge of the white paper.

Spray the plaques with a light coat of acrylic spray. Wrap the plaques in colored tissue paper and have the children present them to the special people for whom they were made.

Letter Holders

Materials

1½ Chinet paper plates per child

green, orange, and yellow construction paper

pink and orange crepe paper

thread

bright-colored felt-tip pen

needlepoint needles

paper cutter

yarn

blue tissue paper

scissors

paper punch

Preparation

Gather the required materials.

Cut some of the paper plates in half. When the half plate is turned upside down and placed on top of the whole plate, a small pocket is formed. Punch holes, evenly spaced, around the outside edge of both plates. Do this for each child's set of plates.

Cut lengths of yarn long enough to be woven in and out of the holes all around the edge.

174

Cut three-inch strips of pink and orange crepe paper and one-inch squares of blue tissue paper. Each child will need two strips of crepe paper and ten to twelve squares of tissue paper. Using a paper cutter, cut thin strips of green construction paper, approximately three inches long. You will need six of these for each child.

Draw several leaf and flower patterns.

Make an example to show the children.

Procedure

Give each child a set of plates, a length of yarn, and a needle. Have him put the plates face to face, match up the holes, and use a threaded needle to go in and out of the holes. Use a wrapping stitch if desired. Tie a tiny bow where the two ends meet. To make a hanging loop, tie a five-inch piece of yarn between the two holes on the top.

Demonstrate how to make the flowers. Have them do the cutting for each flower and then set the pieces aside until they are ready to arrange the flowers on the front of the pocket. They should glue everything down at once. The children will be making two of each type of flower.

For the tulips the children will need to cut out two tulip flowers and four leaves from construction paper. Assemble each flower by gluing down

the stem, placing the flower on the top and the leaves near the bottom of the stem.

Make daffodils by gluing the ends of a piece of crepe paper together. Wrap one end with a length of thread and pull tightly so that the end of the crepe paper is gathered and forms a small cup. Tie two anchoring knots and trim off any excess thread. On the opposite end gently stretch the crepe paper so that the cup opens to form a small bell. The children should cut out two bases for the flowers and four long thin leaves. Glue on the stem and the leaves. The yellow base should be glued to the top of the stem and the small bell to the center of the base.

To make the hyacinths, cut four short leaves and two two-inch stems. Glue on the stems and the leaves. Cup a square of tissue paper around the end of the pencil. To attach each of the tiny cups, apply a small drop of glue at the position desired and push the center of the paper cup down on the drop of glue. Work up from the bottom, attaching five or six flowers to the stem until it is entirely covered.

Have the children arrange their flowers on the front of the pocket. Glue down the flowers.

On the top half of the letter holder write, "To My Mom," or another appropriate saying or greeting with a colored felt-tip marker.

Have the children give the letter holders to their mothers on Mother's Day.

Soap Gifts

Materials

2 small bars of colored soap per child	colored ribbon
2 small biblical pictures per child	scissors
glue	tissue paper
several bottles of clear fingernail polish	ribbon

Preparation

Buy small pictures of Bible scenes. The pictures should be slightly smaller than the bars of soap.

Gather the rest of the materials needed.

Make an example to show the children.

Procedure

Give each child two pictures and two bars of soap. Glue a picture onto the top of each bar of soap.

When the glue has dried, have each child paint the picture with clear nail polish. Each bar of soap should have two layers of polish to make the picture waterproof. Let the polish dry before wrapping.

Wrap each of the bars of soap in tissue paper and tie a pretty bow on top. Have each child give the bars of soap to someone special.

Pomander Balls

Materials

1 apple or orange per child	newspapers
½ yd. of ½" ribbon per child	whole cloves
cinnamon	sewing pins
ginger	1 small bottle of aris powder
small paper bag	

Preparation

Buy the materials listed above. The aris powder can be obtained from a pharmacy.

Cover the worktable with newspapers. Cut the ribbon into nine-inch lengths.

Procedure

Give each child a piece of fruit, a box of cloves, and a length of ribbon. The children should wrap the fruit with the ribbon so that it forms two lines going vertically up the sides. Anchor the ribbon with sewing pins. Tie a loose bow and retie it when finished with the balls.

Press cloves into the fruit until it is completely covered.

Put equal amounts of cinnamon, ginger, and aris powder in a paper bag. Start with enough to cover the bottom of the paper bag and add more if necessary. Put one piece of fruit at a time into the bag, close the top, and shake it until the fruit is completely covered with spices. Take out the fruit and dust off the spices from the ribbon with a brush. Retie the bow. Tie on another piece of ribbon to make a hanger.

Wrap the pomander balls and give them to special people. The balls can be put in a closet or in a drawer. The cloves draw out the moisture from the fruit so the balls will last for a long time. Over a period of time they will lose their spicy fragrance.

If you do this project at Christmas time, read the story of the Magi and of their gifts of frankincense and myrrh for the baby Jesus.

PART 3

Crafts for Intermediate Students

Old Testament

1. Creation

Creation Mural

Materials

large sheets of white butcher paper

blue, black, green, and yellow tempera paint

paper flower pattern (See p. 97.)

dove pattern (See p. 50.)

paintbrushes

scissors

transparent tape

yarn or string

magazines

rubber cement or glue

thumbtacks

colored construction paper

Preparation

Tape several sheets of butcher paper together and place on the floor where the children will have room to work.

Gather necessary materials.

Mix tempera paint.

Procedure

Divide into three groups. Each group will have a project to complete.

Group 1: This group will paint the earth, sky, mountains, sun, moon, stars, grass, trees, etc. on the background paper. For variation, some things such as the sun, moon, and grass, may be cut from construction paper and pasted in place.

Group 2: Using magazines, this group will need to find and cut out pictures of animals, one man, one woman, and plants. Paste these to the mural. This group may also make some flowers to paste on the mural. (See p. 97.)

Group 3: This group will make doves to hang from the ceiling in front of the mural. Follow the instructions found on page 50.

When the mural has been completed, hang it on a wall, using tape or thumbtacks to secure it. Hang the flying doves in front of the mural.

Soap Carving

Materials

1 large bar of soap per child	turpentine
1 paring knife per child	pencils
black model paint	small brushes

Preparation

Have the children bring a bar of soap and a paring knife to class the week you plan to do the lesson or gather all the materials yourself. (See instructions for soap carving in Recipes and Methods at back of book.)

Procedure

Have the children carve some of the animals that God created. Turtles, fish, bunnies, dogs, lions, and butterflies are easily done. Animals with short stubby legs are the easiest to make as legs and fine details are among the hardest things for children to carve.

After the animal has been carved, have the children paint an eye on each side of the head, using a small brush and the black model paint. Clean brushes in turpentine.

Ecology Mural

Materials

large sheet of butcher paper or an old sheet	scissors
	rubber cement
large map of the world (optional)	felt-tip pens
magazines	

Tape the large sheet of butcher paper to the wall. You may want to tape several pieces together to make it larger or use an old sheet instead.

Procedure

Write or stencil across the top of the mural, "God Made the World; Let's Take Care of It." If you have a world map, tape or glue it to the center of the mural. Cut pictures from magazines showing things that God made and for the care of which we should be responsible. You may also show pictures of things for which proper care has not been taken. Glue the pictures on the banner.

Ladybug Pins

Materials

modeling compound	turpentine
black cording	1 medium safety pin per child
1 foil-covered cookie sheet	scissors
small jars of red and black acrylic paint	small brushes

Preparation

Gather necessary materials and make a ladybug pin to show the children.

Procedure

Give each child a small piece of clay. The clay should be kneaded until it is soft. To make the ladybug's head, roll a half-inch ball. Then make a larger ball and flatten it to make the body. Stick the pieces together.

Give each child four one-half-inch pieces of black cording. Turn the ladybug over and push in two pieces of cording for the front legs and two pieces for the back legs.

Give each child a safety pin and have him press the side with the catch on it into the underside of the body.

Bake the ladybugs at 325° for about ten minutes. When they are finished, the clay will be hard. Watch to see that the clay does not become brown.

When the ladybugs have cooled, paint them with red and black acrylic paint.

Snake Puppets

Materials

wool socks

red felt

needles

thread

black buttons

old nylons or other stuffing material

Preparation

Slit the end of each sock across the toe. Cut red felt into an oval to fit the opening you have cut in the toe.

Procedure

Place the red felt into the opening in the sock and with needle and thread stitch around the outside edges so that the felt is sewn into the opening to form the mouth of the snake. Cut a slit in the center of the red felt and put a two-inch strip of red felt into the hole at the center and stitch from the inside to secure. This will make the tongue.

Sew the buttons onto the sock for eyes.

You may want to use markers to make diamonds on the back of the sock.

Put stuffing as far into the top and bottom of the mouth as possible. You will need only a small amount to make the mouth so that it does not wrinkle.

Put your hand into the sock with the fingers in the top of the mouth and the thumb in the bottom. By moving your fingers and thumb you can make the mouth open and close.

2. Noah

Stick Puppets

Materials

old magazines or coloring books

glue

crayons or markers

popsicle sticks

cardboard box

tempera paints and brushes

construction paper

Procedure

From magazines or coloring books, cut people and animals to represent Noah, his family, and the animals on the ark. Mount the pictures on construction paper and cut out again. Color the pictures if necessary. Glue each picture to a popsicle stick.

Make a stage from a cardboard box. Cut off the flaps and lay the box on its side. Paint the inside of the box. Use a knife to make a two-inch slit in the bottom of the box. Support the box on the sides so that the person giving the show can sit under the box and slide the puppets through the slit.

Rainbow Poster

Materials

large piece of blue tagboard	2 yards striped ribbon
cotton balls	brown construction paper
glue	coloring book
old magazines	

Procedure

Cut pictures of Noah and his family from a coloring book. Color them and back them with pieces of construction paper. Cut from the construction paper. Find pictures of animals in magazines and follow the same process.

Cut the ribbon so that it will fit across the top of the tagboard in an arch and glue it to the tagboard. Glue cotton balls to the poster for clouds. If you can find a picture of a dove, place it in the sky, also.

Cut an ark from brown construction paper and glue under the rainbow in the center of the poster. Glue Noah, his family, and the animals onto the poster.

Hang for display.

Box Scene

Materials

small appliance box

construction paper

coloring books with pictures of animals, Noah and his family, and the ark

glue

scissors

paint and brushes

sand

twigs and small branches

cotton balls

newspaper

paint shirts

Procedure

Cut the top flaps off the box. Lay newspaper on the work area. Paint the inside bottom (back of scene) and the sides to make the sky, trees, and land. In the middle, paint part of the mountain top. You may also paint a sun and a rainbow, reaching from the bottom corners across the sky.

Pile some sand in front of the mountain for a three-dimensional effect. Smooth the sand away from the mountain. Put twigs and small branches into the sand to form trees. Glue a few cotton balls in the sky for clouds.

From the coloring books cut Noah, his family, and some animals. Color these pictures, mount them on construction paper, and cut around them. Use the same procedure to make the ark or cut an ark from cardboard and paint it. Place the figures in the sand to look as though they are coming off the ark.

3. The Patriarchs

Abraham's Family Tree

Materials

large sheet of white butcher paper

tempera paints and brushes

25 construction paper circles

glue

Bibles

green and brown crayons

markers

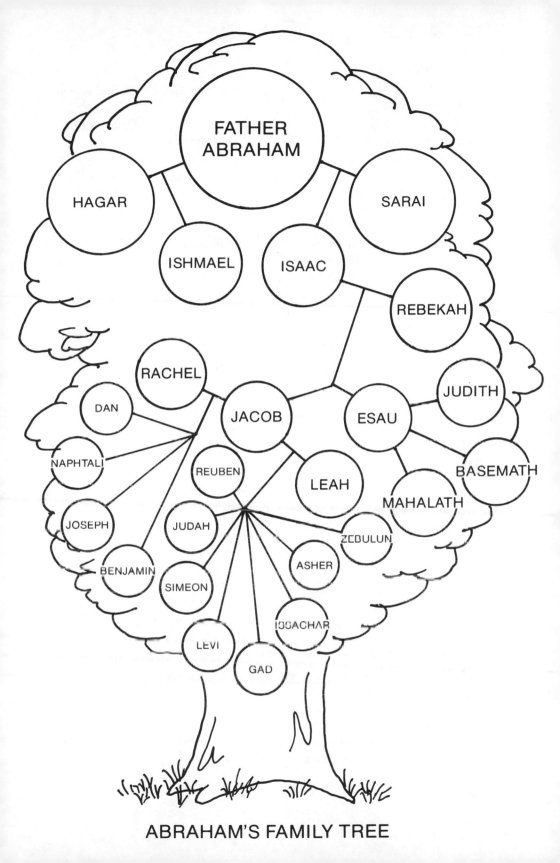

ABRAHAM'S FAMILY TREE

Procedure

On the white butcher paper, outline a large tree. Color the trunk brown and the tree green.

Cut several different size circles from construction paper. On a large one print, "Father Abraham." Place it at the top of the tree. Have the children follow the guide below to find the names to write in the other circles. After they have filled in all the circles attach them to the tree and draw lines between them to show who is related to whom.

> Abraham
> Abraham's wives (Gen. 16:1-2)
> Hagar's son (Gen. 16:15)
> Sarai's son (Gen. 21:3)
> Isaac's wife (Gen. 24:67)
> Isaac's sons (Gen. 25:24-26)
> Esau's wives (Gen. 26:34; 28:9)
> Jacob's wives (Gen. 29:23, 28)
> Jacob's children (Gen. 35:23-26)

Weaving on a String Loom (Jacob)

Materials

1 7" × 5" sheet of heavy cardboard per child
7' of light-colored medium-weight yarn per child for warp strings
several skeins of medium-weight yarn in various colors for woof strings
several pocket combs with broadly-spaced teeth
yarn needles or tiny shuttles made out of cardboard
scissors

Preparation

Buy colors of yarn that look good together. You may use various textures of yarn. Gather the rest of the materials. Make a loom and weave several rows of yarn so that the children will be able to see toward what they will be working.

Procedure

Give each child a piece of cardboard and have him cut slits one-half inch deep and one-half inch apart. Do this along both of the five-inch sides of the loom. Then give each child a seven-foot length of yarn. This will be used to make the warp strings. Start at the top of the loom, hooking the end of the yarn into the first slit. Leave approximately two inches of yarn hanging loose at the end to tie onto when starting to weave. Stretch the yarn to the opposite end of the loom, press the yarn into the bottom slit, move it over to the next slit, and then bring it up to the top of the loom again. All cross-overs should be done on the back side of the loom. Continue doing this until the last slit has been reached. The children should end up on the corner diagonal to where they started. The warp strings should be tight so that they will form a firm backing for the material being woven.

Have each child pull several feet of yarn from a skein with which he wishes to start. Thread one end of the yarn through a needle. Tie the opposite end of the length of yarn onto one of the hanging warp strings. To weave this yarn, or woof thread as it is called, go under the warp thread nearest to the tie-on string. Go over the next thread. Continue going under and over the threads until the end of the loom is reached. Start the next row opposite of the way the first row ended. For example, if the woof string went under the last warp string, begin by putting the woof string over the warp string. Continue working back toward the opposite end of the loom.

The children should use a comb or fork to press the second row of woof threads next to the first row. The closer the woof threads are to each other, the stronger will be the material.

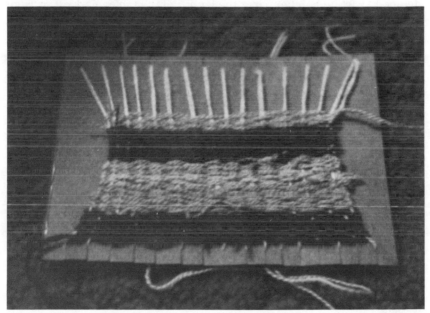

When finished, have the children tie the end of the woof yarn onto the hanging end of the warp thread at the end of the loom. To remove the square of material, slip the warp strings off of each end of the loom.

To make a purse, fold the material in half, tucking in the warp string loops. Sew the sides together.

To make a doll blanket for the nursery, crochet around the squares and then crochet the squares together.

T.V. Story of Jacob

Materials

small appliance box	white butcher paper
knife	markers or crayons
contact paper	tape
2 dowels	

Procedure

Cut off the top flaps of the box. On one side cut out a square hole. Cover the box with contact paper.

Read about the life of Jacob and decide which scenes you want to depict. Lay white butcher paper the length of the table. Mark off sections for the different scenes. Number the sections and then let each child draw one of the scenes. Tape the ends of the paper to dowels and roll the entire story from the right end to the left.

Place the story into the box so that the first picture is lined up in front of the cut-out area. As you tell the story, roll the paper from left to right.

This is a good activity for older children to make and present to younger children.

Pillowcase Patchwork Coats (Joseph)

Materials

1 pillowcase per coat	needle and thread (optional)
scraps of material	darning needles and yarn
glue	waxed paper
scissors	

188

Procedure

Cut the pillowcase up the middle of the front to the top. At the top cut an oval to form the neck opening. Try on the coat and mark where to cut the arm holes on the sides. Slip it off and cut out the arm holes. Lay the pillowcase flat on the work area.

Cut the scraps of material into many shapes. Use different colors and patterns. Slip a sheet of waxed paper inside the coat so front and back layers will not be accidentally glued together. Starting with the front of the coat, glue the scraps to the pillowcase, overlapping each piece. Continue until you have finished both sides. Secure the scraps by using the darning needle and yarn. Come up through the middle of each piece and clip the yarn, leaving about two inches of yarn on both ends. Tie as you would a quilt.

Egyptian Headdresses (Joseph)

Materials

tagboard	pencils
scissors	tape
gold spray paint	green yarn
black and green tempera paint and brushes	newspaper
	paint shirts

Preparation

Before class make one of each of the pieces to be used as a pattern. (Refer to the diagram.)

Procedure

To make the cone shape, place the pattern on tagboard and cut a large circle. Spray paint the circle gold.

Cut a slit to the center and pull one end over the other to form a cone. Staple the ends to secure.

Cut the two side pieces from the tagboard. Paint them black. Cut a slit along each side of the cone and insert the tabs of the side pieces. Tape on the inside.

With a pencil draw circles around the cone. Paint every other ring green.

Punch two holes in the sides of the cone at the bottom and tie a piece of yarn through the hole on each side. Tie these under the chin to hold on the headdress.

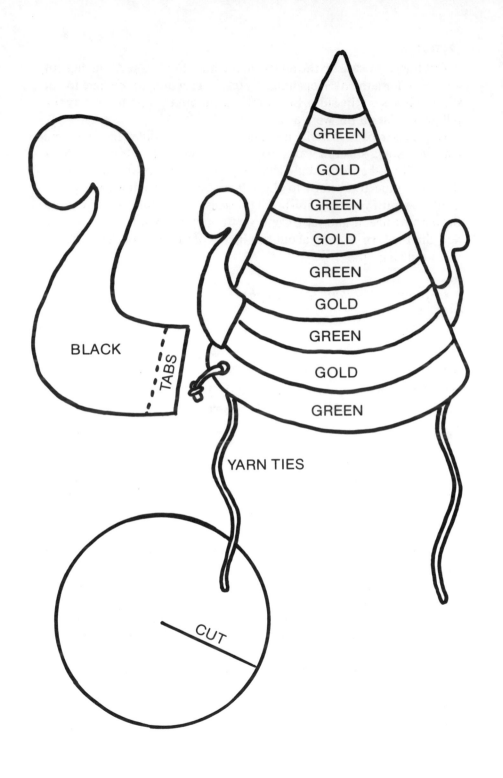

4. Moses

Crayon Etching (The Burning Bush)

Materials
white construction paper
fluorescent crayons
black crayons
bobby pins, nail files, or nails

Procedure
Scribble heavily on white construction paper with different colors of fluorescent crayons.

Color over the other colors with a black crayon. Cover heavily and completely.

Use a nail, bobby pins, or a nail file to etch a burning bush. As you scrape away the black color, the other colors will stand out.

Freedom Boxes (The Exodus)

Materials
1 cigar box per child	yarn
magazines	felt-tip pens
scissors	rubber cement
1 3" × 5" sheet of white construction paper per child	glue

Preparation
Gather the required materials. Cigar boxes may be obtained from a drugstore. Magazines such as *Time*, *Newsweek*, and other news-reporting journals make excellent sources for this type of picture.

Procedure
Have the children go through the magazines and cut out pictures that represent freedom or absence of freedom. They will need several pictures to cover their boxes.

Give each child a white rectangle and have him write on it, "Freedom Is Precious," or any other appropriate saying. Glue the pictures so that they cover the sides, the top, and the inside lid of the box. When the pictures have been attached, glue the rectangle on the lid. Cut a length of yarn long enough to go around the perimeter of the sheet with the saying on it. Glue the yarn around the edge.

The children can put their school supplies, trinkets, or personal possessions in their boxes.

T.V. Story (Crossing the Red Sea)

Materials

small appliance box	white butcher paper
knife	markers or crayons
contact paper	tape
2 dowels	

Procedure

Adapt the directions for the T.V. Story of Jacob on p. 188 to make a T.V. story of Moses and the Israelites crossing the Red Sea.

Commandment Slates

Materials

2 12″ × 18″ sheets of light-colored construction paper or tagboard per child	rulers
	scissors
2-3 12″ × 18″ patterns of the clay tablets	paper punch
	yarn
black felt-tip pens	pencils
crayons	

Preparation

Before class, cut the tagboard into tablet shapes. These need to be large enough for the children to write all Ten Commandments. Making extremely large tablets also makes the lesson more impressive for the children. Ahead of time, write the Ten Commandments on a blackboard or on butcher paper for the children to copy.

Procedure

Give each child two large sheets of construction paper. Have him trace around the tagboard patterns and cut out his tablets.

Next use a ruler to draw lines one inch apart from where the arched section of the tablet stops down to the bottom.

With a pencil write, "The Ten," on one tablet and, "Commandments," on the other, forming a semicircle across the top of the arch (by using a pencil the child can erase if he makes a mistake). Trace over the pencil marks with a crayon.

Write the simplified commandments on the tablets. The first five commandments go on the first tablet and the last five commandments go on the second tablet. The writing should be done with a black felt-tip pen.

Punch two holes on the inside edge of each tablet and tie together with yarn, forming a book.

Commandment Banners

Materials

popsicle sticks	scissors
construction paper	glue
felt-tip markers	copy of simplified Ten Commandments
macramé cord	

Procedure

Using one stick as a pattern, trace around it on construction paper eleven times. On one of the papers print, "The Ten Commandments," and on each of the other ten papers print one of the commandments. Cut each paper from the construction paper. Glue each of these to a stick and let dry.

Glue two sticks together for each of the two sides of the banner.

Put glue on the ends of the stick that says, "The Ten Commandments," and lay it at the top across the side sticks. Continue in this manner until you have all of the commandments attached to the side sticks in order. Let dry.

Turn the banner over and measure a piece of the cord to go all the way around the banner, leaving six inches in a loop at the top. Run a line of glue up the left side and lay the cord on it. Loop six inches at the top and then continue to run the glue and the cord down the right side. Let dry. You may wish to place a heavy object on top to make sure the cord adheres.

5. Historical Books

Papier-mâché Ram Horns

Materials

1 2' square of tagboard per child	paint shirts
newspaper	stapler
flour	paints and brushes
salt	tape
water	

Preparation

Cover the work area with newspaper. Mix the papier-mâché paste according to the directions found in Recipes and Methods at the back of the book. Tear newspaper into strips.

Procedure

Cut the tagboard into two-foot squares and roll into cone shapes. Cut off the excess at the top and bottom to make circular openings. Staple.

Cover the cones with papier-mâché, keeping the layers flat and smooth. Let dry completely.

When dry, mix the paint (tempera paint is best), and paint the horns a light earth tone. Let the paint dry and then use other colors to make designs on the horns.

Brick Doorstops

Materials

1 brick per child	several yards of white felt
yellow felt-tip markers	tacky glue
modeling compound	cookie sheets
toothpicks	small paintbrushes
acrylic paints	

Preparation

Make a paper pattern for the felt brick covers. Cover the bricks as you would wrap a present. Cut one piece of felt per child.

Make an example to show the children.

Procedure

Give each child enough clay to make a mouse to sit on his brick of cheese doorstop. Knead the clay until it is pliable. With half the clay, form a mouse body two inches high. Model legs and set aside. Roll half of the remaining clay into a small ball for the head. Pinch out a nose and press in the eyes. Make a shallow cut below the nose for a mouth and pull the lower lip down. Make ears and attach by moistening the clay. Use half a toothpick to join the head and body. Smooth out the clay where the head and body join to form the neck. Roll a long tail out of the remaining clay. Attach and slightly curl the tail. Position legs.

Form a piece of clay to look like cheese and place in the mouse's front paws.

Bake at 325° for fifteen to twenty minutes or until the clay is hard. While the clay mice are baking, have the children color the white felt to look like Swiss cheese. Draw large and small circles on one side of the felt. Fill in the areas between the circles with a felt-tip marker. Wrap the brick with the colored felt. Secure the felt to the brick with glue.

Paint the cooled mice with acrylic paint. When dry, glue the mice onto the bricks of cheese.

Coat of Arms

Materials

1' × 1' pieces of plywood	polyurethane coating
paint and brushes	sandpaper
stain	white paper

Preparation

If you have a jigsaw and a lathe, you may want to cut the wood into shield shapes. If not, simply leave square.

Procedure

Sand the wood until smooth. Stain or paint it any color. Let dry.

While the paint is drying, draw your design on white paper. You may want to research some of the children's families in advance to find their official coats of arms. Check your local library for a good book on the subject. If you can't find a coat of arms for each family, design your own. When you have an exact design, transfer it to the front of the wood and use markers or paint to color it. Let dry. Brush with polyurethane coating and let dry.

Cartooning of Samson—Delilah Story

Materials
1 long sheet of butcher or freezer paper
pencils
crayons or felt-tip pens

Preparation
Cut a sheet of butcher paper approximately seventy-two inches long. Divide the paper into eight sections. Have crayons, felt-tip pens, and pencils ready to use.

Procedure
Divide the class into eight sections. Have the groups decide on which picture they wish to work. Include pictures of Samson swinging a lion by the tail, Samson carrying the gates of the city on his shoulder, the beautiful Delilah, the cutting of Samson's hair, Samson being carried off in chains, Samson working the grinding wheel, Samson knocking down the pillars, and the auditorium roof crashing down. Draw the pictures in chronological order.

When the outline of the characters has been drawn, the children should color the pictures with crayons or felt-tip pens.

Hang the cartoon series on a wall when finished.

Shields

Materials
tagboard
paper punch
butcher paper
markers
jute

Procedure
Use butcher paper to make a pattern of a large shield. Lay the pattern on the tagboard and draw around it. Cut it from the tagboard. With the paper punch make holes all the way around the shield about two inches in from the edges. Weave the jute in and out of the holes and tie the two ends at the top.

196

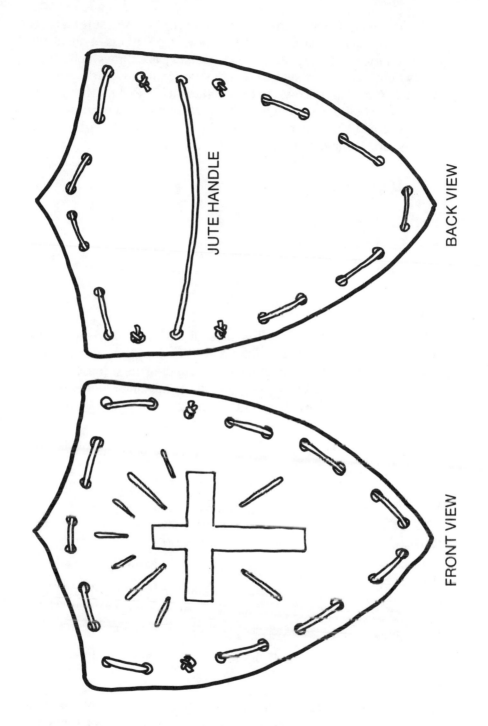

JUTE HANDLE

BACK VIEW

FRONT VIEW

Six inches down from each top corner skip one hole. Measure and cut a piece of the jute to run from side to side with an excess of about two inches on each end. Tie a knot in one end and place through one of the empty holes, using the knot to secure it so it will not slip completely through. Run the jute across the back of the shield and slip it through the other empty hole across from the first. Tie a knot to secure on that end. This piece will be the handle for holding up the shield. With markers create your own design on the front of the shield.

Slings

Materials
heavy material (leather, upholstery material, burlap, vinyl)
paper punch
leather shoestrings

Procedure
Cut an eight-by-four-inch strip of material. Punch a hole in each corner at least one-half inch from the edges. Tie a shoestring on each corner.

Use the slings outdoors in an open field. Holding the strings loosely in one hand place a small rock in the middle of the sling. Move arm in a circular motion and release one of the strings.

Model Church

Materials

1 medium-sized box	scissors
white spray paint	carpet scraps
tissue paper	small boxes
construction paper	white scrap material
clay	tape
glue	

Preparation
Cut the top off the box. Spray paint the outside and the inside.

Procedure
Cut two arched windows on each side. On the part you cut out, draw heavy black lines to form squares and cut between the lines. Cut small

198

strips of tissue paper and glue to the cut-out parts of the windows. Reattach to church with tape.

On the outside of the church draw and color in bricks and bushes.

In the middle of one end draw double doors. Cut across the top and down the middle. Fold the doors back to open.

Cut carpet to fit the inside of the box. Cover small boxes with brown construction paper to make the pews, altar, and pulpit.

Make the altar linens from white material. You may want to draw a design on it.

Use clay to make the cross, chalice, candlesticks, etc.

Crown Pincushions (Esther)

Materials

tagboard	red velvet
glue	stuffing
sequins	stapler
rickrack or gold cording	pencils and ruler
scissors	needle and thread

Procedure

Cut a strip of tagboard ten inches long and four inches wide. Starting two inches from each end, use a ruler and pencil to make the points of the crown. Cut away the area between the points. Staple the ends of the strip together to form a circle. Glue gold cording or rickrack along the tips and base. Glue sequins around the middle.

Cut a ten-inch square of red velvet. Cup the velvet in one hand with the wrong side up and place the stuffing into the center. (Add enough stuffing to make the pincushion hard.) Gather the ends and sew them together tightly to hold the stuffing. Place the red velvet ball into the middle of the crown and stick some straight pins in it.

Glove Puppets (Esther)

Materials

1 white or light-colored glove per child	black, brown, and gray yarn
scraps of red, pink, black, blue, and yellow felt	scissors
	embroidery needles
several cotton balls per child	glue
white thread	

Preparation

Have each child bring an old glove from home. Gather the rest of the materials.

Find a story of Esther and how she saved the Jewish people.

Make an example if you feel it would be helpful.

Procedure

Read the story of Esther to the children. Have each child take several cotton balls and divide them to make five small balls. Stuff the balls into the top of each of the fingers of the glove. Tie a thread just below each of the balls to secure. Cut the fingers off each glove.

Use scraps of felt to make the faces of five figures in the story about Esther. Esther, the king, Haman, Mordecai, and Esther's maid.

Hair can be made by sewing three-inch stands of the appropriate color yarn into the top of the head of each figure. The women's hair should not be trimmed but tied back. The men's hair should be cut. Esther, Haman, and the servant should have black or brown hair. The king and Mordecai should have gray hair.

Make miniature crowns for Esther and the king from construction paper or yellow felt. Secure the crowns to the heads of Esther and the king with a few drops of glue.

When finished, have five children present a short skit of Esther's story. Use a puppet stage with a background of a dining room in the castle.

6. Wisdom Books

Job's Peace Symbols

Materials

1 sheet of sandpaper per child	crayons
1 sheet of white typing paper per child	scissors
iron and ironing board	paste
1 10" × 8" sheet of light-colored construction paper per child	flower patterns
felt-tip pens	

Preparation

Gather the required materials and make a sample card.
Set up an ironing area.

Procedure

Give each child a sheet of sandpaper and his choice of a crayon. The children should rub the crayons over the sandpaper, pressing down hard, until the entire sheet has been covered. When the sandpaper is ready, turn it face down on a sheet of white paper and use the iron to melt the crayon onto the paper. You will see that the texture of the sandpaper has been transferred onto the white paper.

Have the children trace six small flowers (from your own pattern) onto their colored sheet. Cut out and paste the flowers in a pleasant design onto the front of a sheet of folded construction paper. The card may open on the side or at the top. Using a felt-tip pen, the children should write, "May Our Love for One Another Bring Peace to All," "Peace Be with You," or any other appropriate saying emphasizing peace. Inside the cards, the children may write a poem.

Encourage the children to give their cards to a special friend or relative.

Psalm Books

Materials

1 8½" × 6" sheet of light-colored construction paper per child

picture of David playing the harp, sheep in a meadow, or something else drawn from the Psalms

stapler

ditto or typing paper

chalk or crayons

scissors

fine-point, felt-tip pens

ditto masters

fixative spray if using chalk

rubber cement

Preparation

Cut the sheets of construction paper to the proper size. Copy the outline of a picture of David, the sheep, or whatever you are going to use on the ditto master. The picture should be no larger than five by four inches in size. Run the ditto onto white paper. You will need one per booklet being made. Also duplicate the Psalms that the children are going to put in their booklets. Gather the rest of the materials and make an example.

Procedure

To decorate the construction paper cover, the children will need to cut a circle around the dittoed picture. They should color in the picture, using chalk or crayons. If using chalk, paste the picture on first. Spray with a fixative spray to protect the colors from smudging. When finished, the children may write a title on their books, such as, "Our Book of Psalms," "David's Psalms for Us," or something similar.

You may want to include the following Psalms in the booklets: Psalm 3:5-8; 23:1-2; 47; 67:1-4; 84:1-4; 96:1-2; 100:4; 103:20-22; 118:24; 127:3-5; 150:1-2.

Proverb Trees

Materials

large sheet of butcher paper

markers

crayons

Bibles

construction paper

Procedure

Cut a pattern of a teardrop shape out of construction paper. Draw around the pattern on several colors of construction paper and cut out the teardrops.

Make a construction paper tree trunk and glue it to the butcher paper.

Scatter and glue the teardrop-shaped leaves at the top of the trunk. Overlap some of them and have others appear to be falling.

With markers make grass and flowers at the base of the tree.

Use fine-tip markers to write proverbs on the leaves.

You may want to use this as a memory lesson. Add a proverb each time a child learns one. If you do this, write the name of the child under the proverb.

Nameplates

Materials

1 16″ × 7″ sheet of light blue construction paper per child

blue or red felt-tip pens

yellow, orange, and green felt squares

patterns of stems, leaves, flower heads, and the sun

cardboard or tagboard

glue

scissors

pencils

rulers

Preparation

Cut the sheets of paper to the designated size. Draw and cut out several of each of the pattern pieces. Make a nameplate to use for an example.

Procedure

Give each child a sheet of light blue paper. Fold the paper in half lengthwise and then fold lengthwise again. Unfold and make it into a triangle, overlapping the ends. Mark which side will be the front.

Unfold and, using a ruler and pencil, lightly mark three lines one-half inch down from the top and one-half inch apart on the front side. Lightly print, "This Is the Day Which the Lord Hath Made," using the lines as guides. Use a felt-tip pen to carefully go over the letters.

Using the patterns for the flowers and the sun, cut out the pieces from felt. Glue three to four flowers across the bottom of the front just below the verse. Glue one flower on the backside.

If the child intends to use the plate himself, have him print his name on the back next to the flower. If he wants to give the plate away, he should print, "To ——— From ———," next to the flower.

When all the writing and pasting has been completed, fold the paper back into its triangular form and glue the two bottom flaps together.

7. The Prophets

Three-dimensional Mural (Jonah)

Materials

1 5′ sheet of butcher paper	pencils
construction paper	felt-tip pens
scissors	other materials, such as scraps of
paste	cloth, yarn, sandpaper, etc.

Procedure

Read the story of Jonah. Divide the class into five groups and give each group a part of the story to depict. The five predominant areas of the story are: Jonah being thrown off the ship into the sea, the whale swallowing Jonah, Jonah preaching to the people of Nineveh, God making the vine grow to shade Jonah, and Jonah sitting by the dead vine. These are vivid scenes which can easily be depicted by the children.

Each group should discuss how to illustrate their scene three-dimensionally. Each picture should be approximately one foot wide.

While the children are discussing, divide the strip of butcher paper into five sections. Write a title at the top of each section for each part of the story such as "They Threw Jonah Off," "The Whale Swallowed Jonah," "Jonah Tried to Save Them," "God Felt Sorry for Jonah," and "Should I Not Spare Nineveh?" If the children work hard they should be able to finish the mural in one session.

Hang up the mural in a prominent place.

Pop-up Whales (Jonah)

Materials

8" × 5" sheets of black or gray construction paper

8" × 4" sheets of black or gray construction paper

4" × 4" sheets of red construction paper

2 4" × 5" sheets of white construction paper per child

2 white circles for the eyes per child

tagboard

scissors

Preparation

Using the patterns on page 206, trace parts of the whale on tagboard and cut out.

Procedure

Give the children the black or gray construction paper and have them use the patterns to draw the outside parts of the whale. Use white paper for the teeth and red paper for the tongue. Use the white paper and a paper punch to make the eyes.

Put the mouth pieces together first. Fold the teeth up on the dotted lines. Paste the larger section of teeth to the underside of the top section. Paste the smaller section of teeth to the top side of the bottom section. Paste the tongue over the bottom set of teeth.

Make a large black dot slightly off center in the white eyes and paste an eye on each side of the whale's head. Allow the pieces to dry.

205

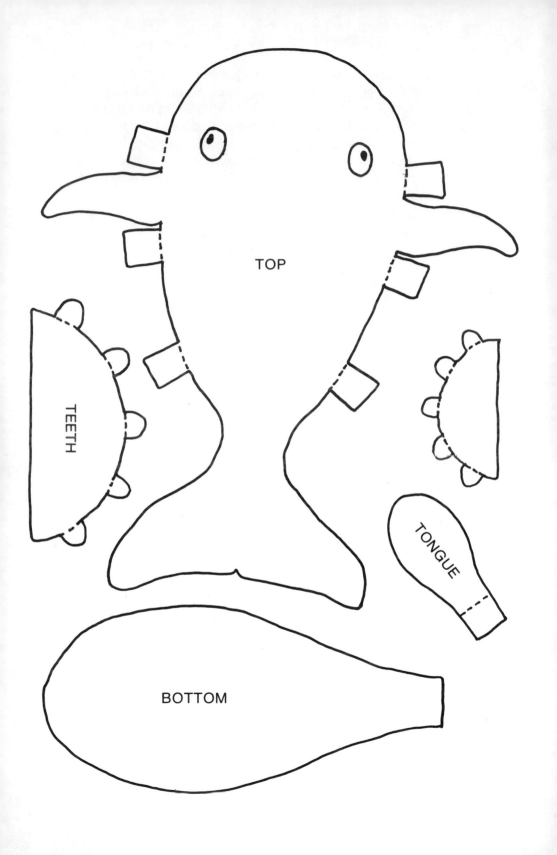

TOP

TEETH

TONGUE

BOTTOM

Attach the top section of the whale to the bottom section by applying glue to the underside of the tabs and folding them over the outside of the bottom section. Allow the top section to curve over the bottom section. Hold the parts together until the glue is dry. Then the flippers and the tail may be gently folded up.

FINISHED WHALE

New Testament Crafts

1. Birth and Childhood of Jesus

Wooden Spoon Scenes

Materials

wooden spoons	eye screws
tempera paints and brushes	glue
decals or old Christmas cards	newspaper

Procedure

Cover the work area with newspaper. Paint the spoons any color you wish.

Use the decals according to the manufacturer's instructions or cut out small pictures from old Christmas cards and glue to the center of the spoon.

Drill a small hole through the top of the handle and add the eye screw. Hang to display.

Treetop Angels

Materials

white construction paper	round styrofoam balls
stapler	plastic eyes
glue	yellow yarn
white lace or chiffon material	pipe cleaners
gold trim	markers

Procedure

Cut the construction paper into eight-inch squares. Roll each square into a cone shape and staple. Cut off any excess. Cut a piece of the chiffon material and drape it over the cone. Cut a small hole where the point of the cone touches the material. Pull the material down over the cone and place a small amount of glue around the neck to secure.

From white construction paper, cut out two arms and hands which look bent as if held in prayer. Glue material onto arms and color the hands pink. Glue an arm to each side of the body.

Cut out two wings and cover with glue. Sprinkle gold glitter over the glue. Do this for both sides of the wings. Glue wings to the back of the angel.

With the markers draw a nose and mouth on the styrofoam ball. Glue on the plastic eyes. Cut yarn for hair and glue onto the ball.

Place the ball on top of the cone and make a mark on the underside where the pieces touch. Remove the ball and on the spot marked make a small hole so that it will fit over the cone. Put a small amount of glue into the hole and attach the ball to the cone.

Around the neck and bottom edge of the dress apply a small line of glue and attach gold rickrack.

To make a halo, glue rickrack onto a pipe cleaner. Bend the pipe cleaner into a circle, leaving one end straight to push into the back of the head.

Put the angel over the top part of a Christmas tree.

Popsicle Stick Manger

Materials

popsicle sticks

glue

straw

small plastic dolls

Procedure

Cross two popsicle sticks and glue together where they cross. Glue two more sticks in the same manner. These are the legs of the manger. Let dry. Lay the leg pieces one stick length apart. Apply glue to the ends of several popsicle sticks. Starting at the center of the leg pieces, lay the sticks flat and side by side to form one half of the manger. Do the same for the other half. Let dry. You may want to stain the wood.

Place a small amount of straw and the plastic doll into the manger.

210

Spatter-painted Cards or Murals

Materials

coloring book with pictures of the nativity

wallpaper samples

construction paper

fine-mesh wire

old toothbrushes

black tempera paint

markers

newspaper

paint shirts

medium-sized boxes

Procedure

Cut figures of Mary, Joseph, the baby Jesus, and some animals from coloring books or old Christmas cards.

Lay newspaper on the work area. Choose a sheet of construction paper for background. Lay the paper in a box and arrange the figures on the paper. Place the wire screen over the box, gently dip a toothbrush into paint, and rub the brush over the screen. (Do not use too much paint as it will fall in globs on the paper.) Remove the wire and carefully take the picture out of the box. (You may want to let it dry before trying to move it.)

Carefully lift the figures from the paper. Use markers to draw a stable around the figures. If you are making cards cut wallpaper twice the width of the picture, fold, and glue the picture on the inside. On the outside print, "Merry Christmas." Sign your name inside.

Silhouettes

Materials

old Christmas cards with pictures of Mary sitting on a donkey and Joseph walking

10" × 12" sheets of black construction paper

10" × 12" sheets of light-colored construction paper

water colors

brushes

water

scissors

glue or paste

Preparation

Ask members of your church for old Christmas cards with the above mentioned scene.

Procedure

Cut out the figures of Mary and Joseph.

On light-colored construction paper paint a background scene with water colors.

If you have enough figures for each child, you may wish to glue or paste the figures directly to the pictures. If not, lay the figures on black paper and trace around them to make a silhouette. Carefully cut out the silhouettes and glue them to the background picture.

Driedals

Materials

box pattern	scissors
letter patterns	glue
construction paper	stapler
sharpened pencils or dowels	markers
tagboard	ditto master

Preparation

Trace the driedal pattern and letter patterns onto the ditto master and duplicate.

Procedure

Cut out the driedal pattern and trace it onto tagboard. Cut it from the tagboard. Fold on the dotted lines and tape together. Cut a small hole (slightly smaller than the handle you plan to use) through the center of the top and bottom of the box.

Cut out and trace the letter patterns onto construction paper. Cut out and paste the letters onto the sides of the driedal.

Use a four-inch dowel sharpened on one end for the handle. Insert through the holes point down.

To play the game

Give all the children equal amounts of candy, raisins, nuts, etc. One child will spin the top. Before spinning you will need to decide what the letters represent. For example, if the driedal lands on the ש, the child spinning will give one nut to each of the other players; if it lands on the ה everyone gives the spinner one nut. Make rules for each of the letters and let each child have a turn spinning. After a certain time limit call the game. The player with the most items wins.

212

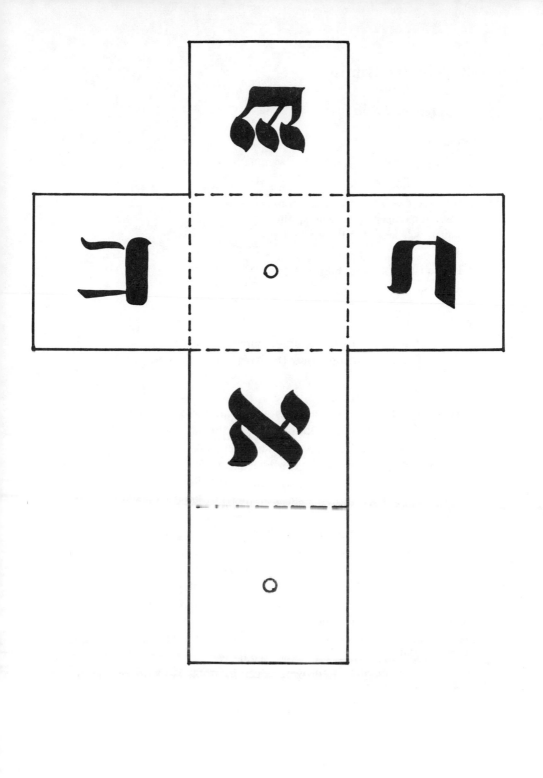

2. John the Baptist

Baptismal Font

Materials

1 toilet paper tube per child

1 spray can lid per child

2″ to 3″ squares of tan or brown con-struction paper (The size of the square will depend on the size of the lid.)

1 1½″ square of foil per child

1 box of wooden coffee stirrers

light brown tempera paint

tacky glue

pencils

newspapers

scissors

paintbrushes

pliers

Preparation

Gather the materials. Make an example to show the children.
Mix the tempera paint. Cover the work area with newspapers.

Procedure

Give each child a lid from a spray can and a square of brown or tan construction paper. Draw around the top of the lid onto the paper. Cut out the circle and paste it on top of the lid. Set aside.

Apply glue to one end of the cardboard tube. Place the lid upside down and center the glued end of the tube in the middle of the lid. If more glue is needed, apply it around the sides of the tube. Let dry for a few minutes.

Measure the length of the coffee stirrers needed to fit on the center tube. Do this by holding a coffee stirrer vertically next to the tube and marking the point on the stick (stirrer) where it reaches the end of the tube. Use the stick to determine the length of the rest of the sticks. Break off the excess from each stick using a pair of pliers. Use the same procedure when measuring the length of the sticks needed to go around the side of the lid. When the children have finished measuring the sticks, glue the sticks to the sides of the tube and to the lid. Let dry for a few minutes, giving the glue a chance to adhere.

Paint the baptismal font brown. Be careful not to get paint on the paper covering the top of the lid. Cut out a circle from foil. Paste the foil to the center of the top of the font. This will represent the basin.

214

3. Calling of the Disciples

Fishers of Men Picture

Materials

white paper
pencils
markers or crayons

Procedure

On the blackboard write, "I Will Make You Fishers of Men." Have the children copy the verse across the top of their papers. They are then to make a picture of what the statement brings to mind. This is a simple but effective craft. Use the pictures as a teaching aid and then display.

4. The Miracle Stories

Wine Jars (Wedding at Cana)

Materials

greenware clay
several rolling pins
moistened cloths
newspapers
7" × 7" squares of cardboard

dull knives
bowls of water
oilcloth or an old sheet
pencils

Preparation

Buy a sack of clay from a ceramic craft shop. Arrangements for firing the jars should be made.

Gather the rest of the materials. Cover the worktable with newspapers and place a cloth on top. Review the procedure for making the jars.

Procedure

Give each child a handful of clay. The clay should be kneaded until it is soft and pliable. Flatten half of the clay into a rounded mound. Using a rolling pin, roll the clay one-quarter inch thick. Cut a two to three-inch circle from the center of the flattened clay. Smooth any cracks with a moistened finger. Place the clay circle on the square of cardboard and cover with a moistened cloth. Gather the scraps and knead them. Add moisture to keep the clay pliable. Roll about one-fourth of the ball into a long rope about one-half inch thick.

Lay the rope around the outside edge of the clay circle. With a moistened finger, smooth the areas where the two pieces join. Continue wrapping the clay rope around the circumference of the jar, laying the rope directly on top of the coil below. As the wall is built, the children will have to use one hand for support when smoothing. While making a new rope cover the jar with a moistened cloth. Three or four ropes will be needed to build a jar approximately four inches tall. The last row should be pushed slightly inward to form the lip of the jar.

When the jar is finished and completely smooth, decorate the outside by lightly drawing a design with a pencil.

Let the jars dry three or four days before firing. If the walls are more than one-quarter inch thick, it may take a few days longer for the pots to dry thoroughly. Have the pots fired. If desired, glaze the pots and fire again.

The wine jars can be used for a vase or a small planter. If they are not glazed, they will not be waterproof.

Braille Cards (The Blind Man)

Materials

1 8″ × 10″ index card per child   1 sheet of graph paper per child
1 medium-sized safety pin per child   felt-tip pens
pencils

Preparation

Make a Braille letter chart like the one on page 53. Think of a few verses that can be used. Gather the required materials.

Procedure

Follow the directions for Braille cards found on page 53.

Jar of "Thankful" Capsules (The Healing of the Lepers)

Materials

1 or 2 large baby food jars

empty gelatin capsules used for medicine (they usually come in quantities of 100)

1 roll of adding machine tape

colored rickrack

glue

fine-tip, felt-tip pens

toothpicks

white construction paper

scissors

Preparation

The empty gelatin capsules can be obtained at a local pharmacy. Get the largest size capsules available. Gather the rest of the materials.

Cut the adding machine tape into one-inch strips. The paper needs to be slightly shorter than the length of the capsule.

Procedure

Give each child several strips of paper on which to write several things for which he is thankful. These might be material possessions, people, or special experiences. Give the child a toothpick and the same number of gelatin capsules as strips. Roll up the strips, using the toothpick as a wrapping tool. Put the rolled strip into a capsule.

The number of jars you will need depends on the number of children in the class and the number of capsules each has made. To prepare the jars, have two children trace around jar lids onto white paper and cut out the circles. With a bright-colored pen have them write, "Thank You, Lord" on the circles. Other children may glue rickrack around the edge of each lid and around the middle of each jar. Glue the paper circles to the lids.

Have the children read a few of the capsules each week to remind them that they should be thankful for the nice things they have in their lives.

This lesson can also be a fun way of learning memory verses. Have each child make a jar of his own. Ditto off the Bible verses on narrow strips of paper. Have the children roll up each strip and put it into a capsule. The jar may be taken home.

Collage

Materials

large sheet of white butcher paper

black marker

old magazines

glue

Procedure

Lay white butcher paper on the work area. Across the top in large block letters write, *"Poems, Prayers, and Promises."* From old magazines cut pictures that represent poems, prayers, or promises. You may write your own poems, prayers, and promises or find some printed poems, prayers, and promises. Glue these onto the paper to make a collage.

Hang up the collage to display.

Bread Figures (Feeding the Five Thousand)

Materials

¼ loaf of frozen bread dough per child

several cookie sheets

shortening and paper towels

small bowl of water

Preparation

Buy the amount of frozen dough that you will need for your class. Thaw the dough in the refrigerator the night before. The dough will be soft and pliable when ready to use. Gather the rest of the materials. Make a small figure as an example and also to check the baking time.

Procedure

Give each child dough and have him knead it to make it workable. While the children are doing this, lightly grease the cookie sheets. Have the children make a dough figure of their choice. Fish, suns, animals, etc., are easily made. When connecting one piece of dough to another piece, the connecting parts should be moistened. Place the dough figures on the cookie sheets, leaving two to three inches between figures.

Place the cookie sheets in 200° ovens. Place a small dish of water in the bottom of each oven. Let the dough rise. This usually takes a half hour. Bake the bread at 350° for approximately thirty minutes or until the dough becomes golden brown.

Take out the figures and let cool. The children can take these home for dinner. The bread should be reheated and then torn apart into individual portions.

Scenes in Hollowed Bread Loaves
(Feeding the Five Thousand)

Materials

⅓ loaf of frozen bread dough per child

paring knives

cotton, green Easter grass, twigs, and other items which might be used to make a scene

newspapers

tiny bows and dried flowers (optional)

7½" × 4" bread pans

plastic figures of people

glue

spray varnish or polyurethane sealer

Preparation

Buy enough frozen bread dough to make one small loaf of bread per child. You will need several small bread pans. Thaw the frozen bread in the refrigerator overnight.

Divide each loaf into thirds. Place in greased bread pans. Turn your oven to warm or 200° and place the bread pans on the top shelf. On the bottom shelf place a small glass bowl of water. Let the dough rise in the oven for approximately one-half hour or until the dough has risen just above the top of the pans. Bake the bread for one-half hour at 350°. Turn off the oven. Remove the bread from the pans and put the loaves back in the oven for fifteen to twenty minutes or until the sides and the top have become extremely hard.

You may want to make a scene in one of the bread loaves to show the children.

Procedure

Give each child a loaf of bread and show him how to cut out one of the sides, leaving approximately one-quarter inch on the remaining side, the top, and the bottom. Take out the rectangular piece and scoop out the insides. All of the bread should be removed up to the hard wall of the loaf. Put the scraps of bread in a plastic bag. Freeze the scraps to use in making bread pudding.

If possible put the loaves of bread back into a warm oven to let the insides dry out thoroughly. Have the children create a scene with the plastic figures and the various items you have provided. Glue the scenes into the bread loaves. To seal the pores of the bread and to give the loaves a shiny appearance, spray the outside of the loaves with polyurethane sealer. A bow and some dried flowers may be attached to the top of each loaf.

Have the children give the loaf of bread as a present to someone special. These make excellent Mother's Day, St. Valentine's Day, or birthday presents.

Bottle Fish (Feeding the Five Thousand)

Materials

1 liquid detergent bottle per child

1 can of light-colored, nonenamel spray paint

dark felt-tip pens

2 1" squares of white construction paper per child

2 ½" squares of black construction paper per child

1 7" × 3" rectangle of red construction paper per child

newspapers

paint shirts

glue

Preparation

Cut off the spouts of the bottles with a knife. Spray paint the bottles. Cut the squares and rectangles of paper.

Procedure

Give each child a bottle. With markers draw in the scales of the fish. Let each side dry before turning the bottles over.

Cut out circles from the squares of black and white paper. Paste a white circle on each side of the wide (bottom) end of the bottle. Paste the black circles in the center of the white circles to make the eyes. Cut a wide, smiling mouth from the red rectangle. Paste this onto the bottle beneath the eyes.

If the children desire, they can flute the tail, cutting the plastic with kitchen shears.

5. Sermon on the Mount

Stained Glass Pictures (Jesus with the Children)

Materials

picture of Jesus with children	black markers
ditto master	masking tape
salad oil	newspaper
crayons	paper towels

Preparation

Find a good picture of Jesus with children. Trace it onto a ditto master and duplicate it.

Lay newspaper on the work area.

Procedure

Cut the picture so that the top is arched and the bottom is straight. Outline with permanent black markers.

Tape the picture to the newspaper to prevent movement while you work on it. Cover the picture with salad oil. Spread the oil with a paper towel. While the paper is wet, color in the picture with crayons. Color heavily, using bright colors. To give the picture more color, turn it over when you are finished and color the other side, making sure to use the same colors in each area as on the first side. Let dry.

When you hang the picture in a window the oil will create a stained glass effect.

Mirrors (Jesus with the Children)

Materials

2″ × 2″ mirrors	decoupage paste
pictures of Jesus with children	glue
6″ × 6″ pieces of plywood	scissors
sandpaper	eye screws
stain	nail

Procedure

Sand the edges of the wood until smooth. Stain the wood on both sides and let dry.

Cut out Jesus and the children separately. Put a large amount of glue onto the back of the mirror and center it on the wood. Put glue on the back of the picture of Jesus and place it in the upper left corner of the wood. Put glue on the backs of the pictures of the children and glue them on the wood so they are arranged around the mirror.

With a nail poke a small hole in the top to start the eye screw. Twist the screw into the wood.

Use decoupage paste to cover all the areas except the mirror. Carefully wipe off any paste that gets on the mirror. Let dry.

Hang up the mirror. By looking into it the child will see that Jesus loves all the children, especially the one in the middle.

6. Prayer

Bread Trays

Materials

pieces of plywood	polyurethane coating
jigsaw	brushes
light or clear wood stain	newspaper
decals	pencils
markers	small stencil letters

Preparation

With a jigsaw cut bread boards (a square with a handle) out of the wood. Stain the wood and let dry.

Procedure

In the middle of the board stencil the words, "Give Us This Day Our Daily Bread." Fill in the lettering with markers.

Following the package instructions, apply decals around the lettering. Let dry and then apply the polyurethane coating with the brushes.

Drill a small hole in the handle to hang.

7. The Parables

Crayon Rubbings of Coins (The Lost Coin)

Materials

white paper

crayons

various denominations of coins

Procedure

See p. 60 for instructions.

Mustard Seed Crosses

Materials

pieces of wood	small picture of Jesus
sandpaper	mustard seeds
dark stain	glue
spray varnish	cross pattern
ruler	construction paper or tagboard (optional)
fine-tip marker	

Procedure

Sand the edges of the wood and stain. Let dry. Spray varnish and let the varnish dry.

Cut out the Celtic cross pattern, center it on the wood, and trace around it with a fine-tip marker.

Glue the picture of Jesus to the center of the cross. To make the plaque more colorful, trace the cross pattern onto bright-colored construction paper or tagboard. Glue the cross to the wood.

Cover the part of the cross that is not covered by the picture with glue. Sprinkle mustard seeds on the glue and shake off the excess.

CUT OUT

PATTERN FOR MUSTARD SEED CROSS

Seed Pictures (The Sower)

Materials

6″ × 6″ white ceramic tile per child
carbon paper
pencils
paint and brushes
glue
coloring books
various assortment of seeds

Procedure

Lay a tile on the work area. Trim a coloring book picture to fit on the tile. Lay the carbon paper face down on the tile and put the picture on top. Tape the edges to secure. Trace the picture onto the tile. You will need to press hard to make sure that all the lines are drawn. Remove the picture and the carbon paper.

Decide which areas you wish to paint and with a small brush carefully paint. Let dry.

Start with one type of seed and place a small amount of glue where you want those seeds. Sprinkle on and shake off the excess. Continue to place the different types of seeds to make a three-dimensional picture. Let dry and handle carefully.

8. Jesus and the Moneychangers

Change Purses

Materials

small plastic containers such as soap bottles
scraps of material
yarn
darning needles
needles and thread
paper punch
glue
markers

Preparation

Cut the tops off the plastic containers.

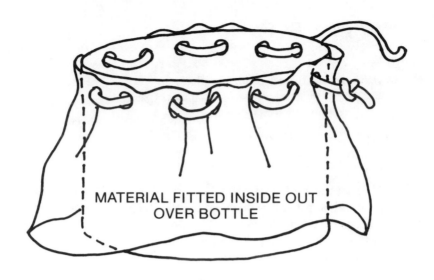

MATERIAL FITTED INSIDE OUT
OVER BOTTLE

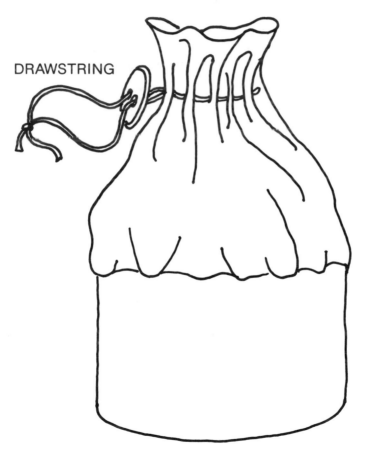

DRAWSTRING

Procedure

Measure and cut a length of material to fit around the container. The strip should be at least six inches wide. Sew the ends together.

Slip the material down over the container inside out. Line up the material with the top edge of the container. Carefully punch holes all around the container through the plastic and the fabric at the same time.

Thread a darning needle with yarn and tie a large knot in the ends. Start at one of the holes and sew all the way around. Tie the ends together when you have completed the sewing.

Turn the material right side out, bringing it above the container. With the darning needle and thread baste around the material about two inches down from the raw edge. Leave about eight inches of yarn on each end. Slip a button with two holes through the yarn and tie the ends of the yarn, positioning the button so it will act as a slide to open and close the purse.

Fold under the raw edge at the top, run a line of glue over the fold, and fold over again.

Use markers to decorate the plastic.

9. Passover

Felt Plaques

Materials

8½″ × 11″ pieces of plywood	scissors
wood stain	glue
purple, brown, white, and gold felt	old church bulletins with chalice and
gold cording	bread pictures

Procedure

Cut the wood to the indicated size and stain. Let dry. Cut a cross eight and one-half inches long by five inches wide from white felt. Cut a three-inch circle from purple felt.

Cut out the bread and chalice pictures and either trace and cut them from brown and white felt or use the pictures directly on the plaque.

Glue the cross in the center of the wood. Glue the circle of purple felt in the center of the cross. Measure and cut the gold cording to go around the outside edge of the circle. Run a thin line of glue on the edge of the circle and secure the cording.

Glue the pictures or the felt pieces of the bread and chalice in the center of the felt circle.

10. Fruit of the Spirit

Mini-Banners (Love)

Materials

solid colors of felt	13″ dowel
gold or silver rickrack or cording	needle and thread
stencil letters	white paper
felt scraps	pencil

Procedure

Draw a cross on white paper and cut it from the paper to use as a pattern. Cut the felt into a twelve-by-fourteen-inch piece. Center the cross pattern on the felt and lightly draw around it. Run a thin line of glue along the outline and run the cording around the cross. Let dry.

On the scrap felt stencil the words, "God's Love—Pass It On." Cut out the letters and put "God's Love—" at the top of the banner in an arch and "Pass It On" across the bottom. Position the letters before gluing them on to make sure they are even.

Fold the top of the banner over one inch to make a casing and sew on the backside. Slip the dowel through the casing. Tie a length of cording to each end of the dowel and hang.

Strings of Fruit

Materials

1-2 squares of felt per child (appropriate colors for fruit)	fruit patterns
	whole allspice, whole cloves, and bits of cinnamon sticks
1-2 squares of dark green felt for leaves	
thread to match colors of felt	sewing needles
1 16″ length of green rug yarn per child	glue
scissors	felt-tip pens

228

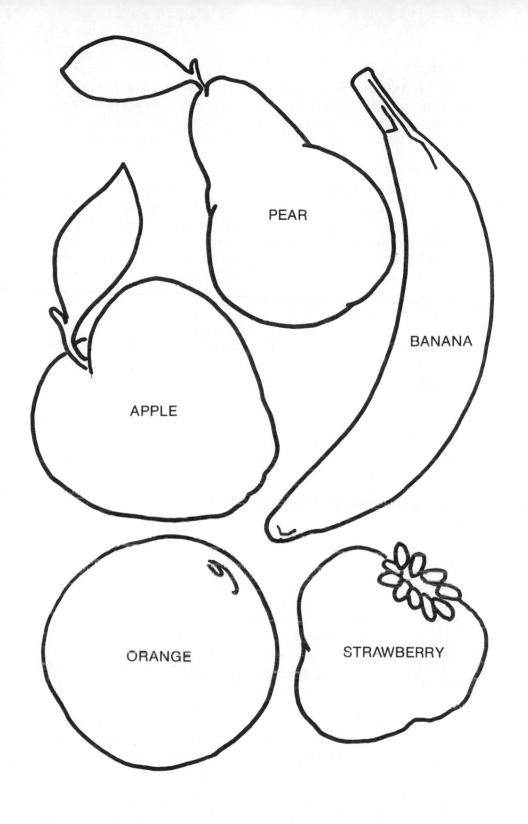

Preparation

Decide if the class will make one type of fruit, such as strawberries, or if they will make several types of fruit. Buy the appropriate color of felt, yarn, and thread. Cut out several of the fruit patterns. Also cut sixteen-inch lengths of yarn. Gather the rest of the materials. Make an example.

Procedure

Have the children cut out two pieces of felt for each piece of fruit being made. The children should sew together the two sections of fruit leaving about two inches open for easy turning. The stitches should be close together and sewn one-half inch from the edge. Turn the fruit right side out. Stuff with a mixture of spices. Sew the pockets closed with a fine stitch. Cut leaves out of green felt. Glue the leaves onto the top of the fruit. Write the name of a fruit of the Spirit on each of the pieces of fruit. Add any necessary dots or lines.

Sew the fruit onto the yarn equal distances apart and leaving one inch of yarn at the top to make a loop for hanging. Four pieces of fruit can be placed on a string.

Hang up the strings of fruit in a kitchen.

Collage

Materials

1 5′ length of butcher paper	thumbtacks
magazines with pictures of people	scissors
rubber cement and white glue	yarn
construction paper	rulers

Preparation

Cut the butcher paper to the required size. Make a mark at the bottom center of the sheet. Mark a point six inches up on each side. Draw a line from each of the side points to the center point. Cut along each of the lines to form a point at the bottom.

Procedure

Have the children cut out pictures of people exhibiting the fruit of the Spirit. Lay the pictures on the banner, cutting and overlapping where necessary. Cut block letters from construction paper for a title for the collage. Using yarn, write the names of the different fruit of the Spirit. Glue the pictures, the title, and the yarn letters on the banner.

Hang the banner up as a reminder to the children and to others that they need to exhibit the fruit of the Spirit.

Joy and Peace Pennants

Materials

pieces of heavy material such as felt, upholstery, or fabric

large stencil letters

glue

scissors

dowels

stapler

construction paper

Procedure

Cut the material into a large triangle (see diagram). On scrap pieces of contrasting colors of construction paper print or use stencils for the words "Joy" or "Peace." Cut out the letters and glue them to the triangle.

Fold over one and one-half inches at the wide end of the pennant to make a casing and place the dowel into the fold. Staple close to the edge to secure the dowel.

Kindness Bulletin

Materials

15″ × 11″ sheets of white or light-colored tagboard or heavy construction paper

1 blue or red 17″ × 13″ sheet of heavy poster board

felt-tip pens

writing paper

pictures of featured people (optional)

2 metal rings

rulers

pencils

paste or rubber cement

paper punch

Preparation

The week before doing this lesson explain to the children that they are going to be reporters. They are to find out what acts of kindness members of the church have been performing. The acts of kindness need not be limited to deeds done for the church. Ask the children to interview people of all ages to find out what they or others have done or are doing for friends, family, neighbors, or the community. For example, someone may be having an anniversary party or shower for someone else. Or someone may be donating something to the church. Make sure the children get all the facts (who, what, when, where, why, and how).

Cut the sheets of tagboard and poster board to the required size. Gather the rest of the materials.

Procedure

Have the children tell what they found during their reporting assignments. Pass out paper and pencils. Tell the children that their articles should give an interesting account of the episode they are reporting; they should also be written concisely with proper grammar. Each child will have a four-by-five-inch page space for their article. Have the children write the articles in final form so that they may be easily copied onto the bulletin.

While the children are working on their articles, make the heading for the first page. Divide each sheet in half lengthwise. Leave one-half inch between the two columns. Draw lines one-half inch apart down the entire sheet of tagboard. The following sheets should be prepared in the same manner but without a heading.

Have the children write their completed articles on the tagboard with colored felt-tip pens. Pictures of the people who did the acts of kindness may be pasted on a space where the article is written. When finished, center the sheets on the poster board with the top of the pages and the top of the poster board even. Punch two holes in the top and thread the pages onto the two metal rings.

Place the kindness bulletin on a table where it may be read by members of the church. Every couple of months, the class may update the bulletin by finding out what acts of kindness have been done since the last issue.

Plastic Pendants

Materials

4″ plastic circles

butterfly pattern

felt-tip markers

nail and hammer

24″ length of light cording

small eyelets

Procedure

Cut out the butterfly pattern and center it on the plastic.

With the nail punch a hole in the top of the plastic and attach the eyelet. Run the cord through the eyelet and tie the ends. Use markers to color the butterfly.

Outline the plastic with a black marker. Write your name above the butterfly.

11. Gifts of the Spirit

Miniature Books of the Bible (Knowledge)

Materials

66 small soap bars
construction paper
cross stickers

felt-tip markers
small boxes

Procedure

Cut the construction paper so that it will fit around the bars of soap. You will need thirty-nine bars and papers for the Old Testament books and twenty-seven of each for the New Testament. (Buy the soap bars from a motel distributor.) Put glue on both sides of each bar of soap and wrap the paper around. Let dry.

Center a cross sticker on the front of each soap book. Along the spine and on the front, print in small letters the name of one of the books of the Bible. Continue until you have a complete set of books.

Make a bookshelf by covering a small box with brown construction paper. Place the soap books into the box so that the lettering on the spines can be seen.

Pennant

Materials

large piece of heavy material
scraps of material
glue
scissors

small picture of each member of the class
large stencil letters
pencil

234

Procedure

Cut the large piece of material into a triangle.

On the scraps of material stencil the words, "We Are the Body." Cut out the letters and glue them to the center of the triangle. Then glue the pictures of the class members around the lettering. You may wish to ask other members of your church or church school to bring in their pictures to add to the pennant.

Hang for display.

12. Communities

Maps of Paul's Journeys

Materials

4 3′ × 2′ pieces of plywood	paint and brushes
world map	thumbtacks
white butcher paper	masking tape
papier-mâché paste	fine-tip markers
toothpicks	paint shirts
construction paper	

Procedure

Cut the wood and sand the edges. Cut a piece of butcher paper to fit one side of the wood. Lay the world map on the table and lay white butcher paper on top. Trace the Mediterranean area onto the paper. Do this process four times.

In the back of most Bibles are maps of Paul's journeys. Study the maps and then divide the class so that each group will cover one of the four journeys.

Mix the papier-mâché. Cover the work area with newspaper and put on paint shirts. Put the white paper on the wood and thumbtack down the edges.

Using small amounts of papier-mâché, build up all the land areas on the maps. Let dry completely.

Mix the paints. Paint the seas and lakes blue, grassy areas green, hills brown, etc.

Make small triangles from construction paper and attach to toothpicks with tape. On each one write the name of a prominent town to which Paul traveled. These may be added with a small dab of glue after the papier-mâché is dried or while it is still wet. On some of the flags you may wish to also add small items of information about what happened to Paul in that place.

The last step is to mark the route of Paul's journey with small pieces of masking tape. In a lower corner make a map legend.

Mite Boxes

Materials

1 cardboard mint box per child (5" long by ¾" wide and 2" deep)

1 8" × 11" sheet of light-colored construction paper per child

13–15 wooden coffee stirrers per child

1 4" × 2" cardboard rectangle per child

black felt-tip pens and markers

1 2½" square of gold burlap per child

glue

paintbrushes

brown tempera paint

newspapers

knife or sharp scissors

Preparation

Purchase the materials needed. Mint boxes can be obtained from a cake decorating store. Coffee stirrers can be found at a restaurant supply store.

Cut the squares of burlap.

Make an example.

Procedure

Have each child wrap a mint box with construction paper in the same way they would wrap a present. Secure with glue.

Using one of the wider sides as the front, make a horizontal coin slot one-fourth of the way down. Just above the coin slot the child should print with a black pen the name of the person who will receive the box.

Make the coin box look like a thatched hut. Glue the coffee stirrers to the front side of the box above and below the space where the name has been printed. Cut a two-by-four-inch rectangle of cardboard to make a flat roof for the house. Glue this to the top of the box.

Paint the entire house with brown tempera paint. Lay it on a newspaper to dry.

While the paint is drying, have the children remove all the strings from the squares of burlap. When the paint is dry, glue the strings to the top of the roof to look like thatched straw. Press the strings down into the glue to make sure that they adhere to the roof.

Using a black marker, draw a door on the front of the house. Let the boxes dry thoroughly before handling.

Have the children take the boxes home to save money for the poor or for missions.

Mite Boxes

Materials

1 small juice can per child	brown chenille pipe cleaners
1 7″ × 4½″ sheet of light brown construction paper per child	brown and black felt-tip pens
	glue
1 4½″ circle of dark brown construction paper per child	sharp knife

Preparation

Have each child bring a small juice can from home.

Cut the sheets and circles.

Cut the pipe cleaners in half. Make an example to show the children.

Procedure

Give each child a sheet of brown paper and have him glue it around the outside of his can. Use the pipe cleaner to make a rounded door. Glue the curved pipe cleaner to the side of the container. With a brown pen make twig-like lines around the entire can. Draw a window on one side of the door. Cut a coin slot across one side about two inches from the top.

Cut a straight line half way into the circle. Form the circle into a cone. Make the cone just large enough to fit the top of the can. Apply a few drops of glue between the two layers of the overlapped paper. Make fine lines around the top with a black felt-tip pen to represent sticks or thatch. Glue the roof onto the top of the can.

Have each child write his name above the doorway of his can.

The children may take the boxes home to save money for the poor or for missions.

Seasonal Crafts

1. Autumn

Leaf Tiles

Materials

2-3 lb. of block clay (fire at about 2000°F) or low-fired red clay (available at most ceramic or craft stores)

2 18" strips of ½" plywood per work area

1 sheet of acetate per work area

oilcloth to cover worktable

leaves and grass

paring knives

2 8" squares of cardboard covered with foil per child

rust colored glaze

brushes

1 rolling pin per work area

1 ruler per work area

spatulas

Preparation

Gather the required materials. A craft store or ceramic shop is a good place to purchase the clay. Most likely you will be able to use their kiln to fire the tiles when ready.

If interesting flowers or trees can be found near your church, let the children gather leaves or flowers at the beginning of class. If not, pick the floral items the day before and put them in a plastic bag to keep them from drying out. Geranium, iris, poppy, and marigold leaves, ferns, tree leaves, and feathery grasses make interesting impressions in the clay.

Keep the clay in a plastic bag until ready to be used. It should be kept moist. Set up work area by covering a table with oilcloth, wrong side up to prevent the clay from sticking.

Procedure

Demonstrate how to make a tile. Knead two or three handfuls of clay. Throw the clay down on the oilcloth a couple of times to work out the air bubbles.

Lay the strips of wood eight inches apart. Slightly flatten the clay and place it in the middle of the sticks. Roll the clay out until it is even with the sticks. You should roll over the clay and sticks to insure that the clay is completely flat and one-half inch thick. The clay should measure approximately sixteen inches long, eight inches wide, and one-half inch thick.

Cut two tiles from the rolled clay. Lay a leaf in the middle of each of the two sections of clay. Cover the clay with a sheet of acetate and use the rolling pin to press the leaves into the clay.

Using a ruler and a paring knife, trim the tiles and cut apart the two sections. Make the edges perfectly straight. Each tile should be eight inches square. With a spatula carefully lift the tiles and place each one onto a foil-covered square. Set in a safe place to dry. Remove the leaves when they begin to dry and curl. It takes about a week for the clay to dry completely.

Fire the tiles once before glazing. Have the children glaze the top of each tile. Three coats are needed to maintain the color. Fire the tiles again.

The tiles make excellent trivets or coasters.

Jute Wreaths

Materials

styrofoam ring (flat, not rounded, top and bottom sides)	tacky glue
natural jute	dried flowers in orange, yellow, gold, etc.
rust-colored jute	silk flowers (optional)
straight pins	

Procedure

Cut a piece of jute forty to fifty yards long. You may need more or less than this amount, depending on the size of the styrofoam ring. Roll the jute into a ball to make it easier with which to work. Put a straight pin through the end of the jute into the ring to secure the end.

Wrap the jute around the styrofoam ring. Push the jute together as you work. When you have the ring completely covered, put glue on the end and secure with a pin.

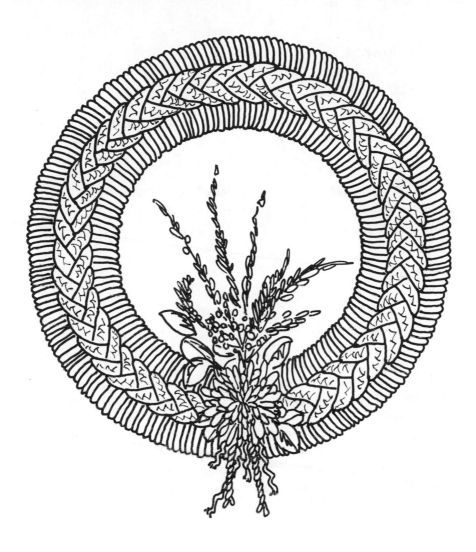

With two pieces of natural jute and one piece of rust-colored jute, measure around the outside of the wreath three times. Cut the jute. Tie the ends together and braid the ropes. Lay the jute-covered ring flat on a table and begin to attach the braid with tacky glue. Use pins to anchor braid securely until glue is dry. Remove pins. Cut off excess braid.

Where the ends of the braid meet, arrange dried and silk flowers. Cut a one-foot piece of natural jute and make a bow. Pin the bow to the front of the flower arrangement.

Hang to display.

2. Halloween

Dried Apple Dolls

This craft will take approximately four weeks to complete since the apples need to dry thoroughly.

Materials

1 large apple per child	thread and sewing needles
paring knives	support rack
large chenille pipe cleaners	1 8″ wooden dowel per child
lemon juice	old nylons
disinfectant	tacky glue
material scraps	scissors
yarn	newspapers
black and flesh-colored felt	

Preparation

Plan to have the children work on their dolls a little each week until they are finished. The body of the doll may be made while the apples are drying, but the children should be careful not to jar the apple from the support rack or to bump the apple while they are working with it.

Gather the materials as needed. Some type of support rack will be needed to keep the apples steady while they are drying. The cup part of an egg carton placed over an empty box works well. In each of the cups punch a hole in which the dowels can stand up.

Procedure

Give each child an apple, a wooden dowel, and a paring knife. Peel the apple. Push the dowel into the bottom part of the apple as far as possible. Decide which side would make the best face. Indentations should be cut into the apple to make the eyes and mouth. Carve out other facial features. When finished, dunk the apples in lemon juice so that they will dry a golden color. Spray with disinfectant. The apples should be left to dry in a well-ventilated area.

After a week the apples should have begun to shrink. Carefully shape the eyes, nose, mouth, and chin. Wrap pipe cleaners around the dowel to make the basic arm and leg structure. Glue into place. While the glue is drying, have the children cut nylons into strips one and one-half inches wide. Dip the strips in glue and wrap around the body structure to make it thicker. The shoulders of the body should start approximately one-half inch below the head. Continue wrapping until the doll's body is finished. Let the dolls dry during the week.

On the third week the children can make clothes for the dolls. Skirts and dresses are the easiest to do. Children who desire to make pants and shirts may need the teacher's help. Allow the children to choose a piece of material. Fold the material in half. To determine the size of the outfit, lay the doll down on the material. With a pencil mark one inch on each side of the arms, the torso, and, if making pants, the legs. A skirt should be flared out from the waist line. There will be two pieces for each section of clothing. Cut the pieces out. Sew the material together using fine stitches along the outside edges. Leave one-quarter inch seam allowance. When the outfit has been sewn together, turn it right side out and try it on the doll. For a decorative touch sew on lace or other types of trim.

On the fourth week have the children cut yarn for hair. To attach the hair spread white glue on the dried apple where the hair line would begin. Press a length of yarn into the wet glue. Continue until the entire head has been covered. If bangs are desired, attach shorter lengths of yarn to the top of the head. For men's hair, use the same basic method as with the bangs. The hair should fall from the center in a circular fashion, covering the entire head. Pull the ends back and roll into a small bun for a female. For men, trim the ends. Braid the yarn to make an Indian doll.

Cut four hand patterns out of flesh-colored felt. Glue two pieces together and attach to the end of an arm. Felt shoes may be made by cutting a sole and two top parts of the shoe. Glue or stitch the outside of the sole and the two top parts together. Stuff with cotton and attach to the leg.

Felt-tip pens can be used to apply color to the eyes and the mouth. A bonnet or hat may be made to give the doll a finished look.

Jack-O-Lanterns

Materials

pumpkins

knives

newspaper

paper and pencil

fine-tip markers

Procedure

Lay newspaper on the work surface. With a pencil draw the pattern for your pumpkin's face on paper. Transfer this design to the pumpkin with markers. Cut the top off the pumpkin and clean out the seeds.

Carve the pumpkin. Leave a thin membrane uncarved for some areas such as the eyebrows.

Place a candle on the inside. When you light the candle the areas you have not carved completely will cast an eerie glow.

3. Thanksgiving

Kitchen Plaques

Materials

5½″ × 7″ pieces of plywood	small macaroni letters
sandpaper	glue
wood stain	pencil
varnish or polyurethane coating	decals

Procedure

Cut the pieces of plywood and sand the rough edges. Stain the wood and let dry. Coat with varnish or polyurethane and let dry again.

Select the decals you wish to use and follow the instructions to apply to the corners or across the top and bottom. Pick out the letters to spell, "Bless This House, O Lord, We Pray; Make It Safe by Night and Day." With the pencil mark the center of the plaque and draw light lines as guides for the lettering. Glue on the letters.

Let dry and hang for display.

Table Runners

Materials

1 light-colored burlap strip 2′ long and 20″ wide per runner	patterns of a cornucopia, loaf of bread, various fruits and vegetables
gold, orange, green, brown, and red felt squares	cardboard
black felt-tip pens	heavy scissors

Preparation

Cut the strips of burlap. Draw and cut out the patterns.

Procedure

Have the children start by cutting the fruit, vegetables, cornucopia, and loaf of bread from felt. Using felt-tip pens, draw in details.

Glue the cornucopia on the burlap. Add the fruit and vegetables as they look best.

Pull out four to five strings along each side of the burlap to make a fringed edge.

These table runners may be made as a gift for the church, a nursing home, or for the children's families.

"Thankful" Boxes

Materials

1 cigar box per child	yarn
old magazines	felt-tip pens
scissors	rubber cement
1 3″ × 5″ sheet of white construction paper per child	glue

Procedure

Follow the instructions for Freedom Boxes on page 191, using pictures of things for which the children are thankful. Write an appropriate caption on the lids of the boxes.

4. Advent—Christmas

Reindeer Glasses

Materials
pattern for glasses
tagboard
stapler
scissors
pencils

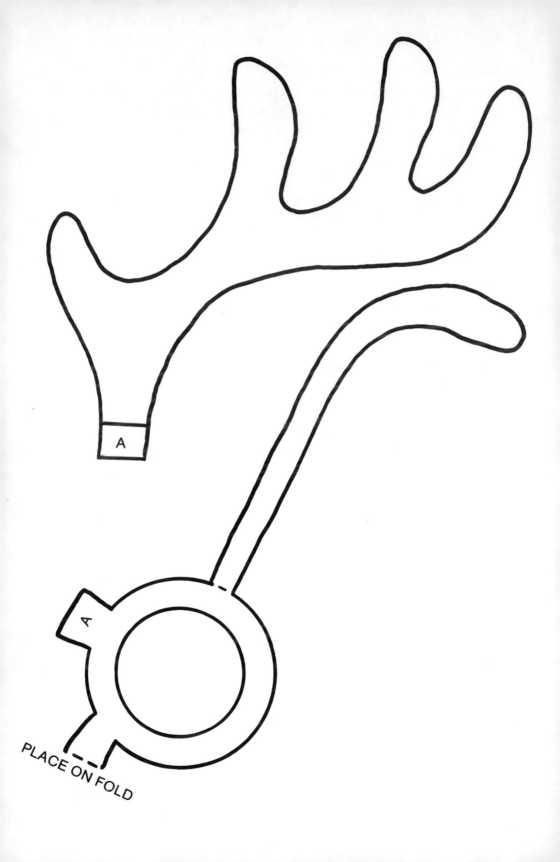

A

A

PLACE ON FOLD

Procedure

Trace and cut out the pattern. Join pattern pieces at point "A." Fold the tagboard and lay the pattern on the fold. Trace and cut out. Unfold the glasses and trim to fit. If the glasses are too big, adjust by cutting from either the bridge or the temples. Staple pieces back together.

Symbolic Tree Ornaments

Materials

book on Christian symbols	small tree
construction paper	glue
markers	scissors
yarn	

Procedure

Make Christmas tree ornaments by drawing symbols that represent Bible characters on construction paper and cutting them from the paper. Be sure to draw them not more than three inches by three inches. Cut background shapes such as triangles, squares, and circles from construction paper and glue the symbols to the background, leaving a border around the symbol.

Add details with markers. Punch a small hole in the top center of the construction paper and thread a piece of yarn through it to make a loop.

The following symbols may be used to represent Bible characters:

Chi-Rho ☧ —Christ
saw and nails—Joseph
lily—Mary
church—Nehemiah
tent—Abraham
apple—Adam and Eve
ark—Noah
coat—Joseph
staff—shepherds
ladder—Jacob
crown—David

Pinecone Wreaths

Materials

tagboard	popsicle sticks
ceramic tile cement	fine silver wire
cardboard	glue
small to medium pinecones	pop can pull tabs
red velvet ribbon	pencils
metallic balls, holly sprigs, and berries	

Procedure

On the tagboard draw a one-foot circle. Draw a smaller circle three inches in from the outside of the circle. Cut out the center of the ring and the excess tagboard around the ring. Use this as a pattern to trace on the heavier cardboard.

Use a popsicle stick to smooth the tile cement on the cardboard ring until it is completely covered on one side. Place pinecones on the cement (use a variety of sizes). Add holly sprigs and berries by wrapping wire around them and attaching to a pinecone. Make a bow from red ribbon and attach it to the wreath with wire.

Glue a pop can pull tab to the back as a hanger.

Candles

Materials

paraffin	old Christmas cards
old pan or teakettle	medium-sized paintbrushes
potholder	waxed twine
old crayons	pencils or short dowels
empty half-gallon milk cartons	washers

Preparation

Lay newspaper on the work area.
Peel off the wrappers from old crayons and put like colors together.

Procedure

Cut pictures from old cards. Measure the cards and cut them to fit the sides of the milk cartons. You will need four cards for each candle.

Tie the washer to the end of the twine. Cut the twine so it is about twelve inches long. Tie the other end around the pencil or dowel. Lower the end with the washer into the milk carton and lay the dowel or pencil across the top. Make sure you have the twine in the center of the carton.

Melt the wax. Each candle will take several blocks of paraffin. To color the wax add the crayons. Pour the melted wax into the carton. Let set and then peel the carton away from the wax.

Melt more wax and brush a small amount on the backside of the cards and stick them to the sides of the candle. Dip the whole candle quickly into the melted wax to form a thin layer over the cards.

Bread Dough Advent Wreaths

Materials

(Each group will need all of the listed materials.)

2 batches of bread dough	flour
foil	3 purple, 1 rose, and 1 white candle
rolling pin, knife, garlic press, small juice glass	green and red food coloring
	cookie sheet
bowls of water	

Preparation

Before class mix and knead the bread dough. (See Recipes and Methods at back of book for bread dough recipe.) Store the dough in plastic bags. Mix one recipe of dough just as stated in the directions. This recipe will be used for making the base of the wreath.

When mixing the second batch of dough, divide the dough mixture as follows: Use one-fourth cup of salt, one-half cup of flour, one-fourth cup of water, and two teaspoons of red food coloring to make the red dough. Use three-fourths cup of salt, one and one-half cups of flour, three-fourths cup of water, and two tablespoons of green food coloring to make the green dough.

Have the children bring in the needed tools for the work session.

Procedure

Divide the class into small groups of three to five children each. On a cookie sheet lay a sheet of foil shiny side up.

Have two children each roll half of the white dough on a floured surface. The dough should be rolled one-fourth inch thick. Using a juice glass, have the children cut fifteen circles from one of the rolled out sections. The circles should be divided into five groups. Seal three circles together by moistening the tops and bottoms. Space these evenly in a circle on a cookie sheet.

Have another child tear apart sheets of foil four inches wide to make "snakes." Each sheet should be crinkled to make a long roll. Several of these will be needed in making the base structure for the wreath. Wind the foil snakes in and out of the dough circles.

Have another child roll out another sheet of white dough a little thicker than the first sheets. Strips one inch wide should be cut from this sheet of dough. The children should cover the foil with the strips of dough, sealing the ends and edges with a moistened finger. The tops and sides should be completely covered.

Another child should roll out approximately half of the green dough and cut out five circles with a juice glass. Put one green circle on top of each of the five white circles, sealing it to the circle beneath and to the sides.

Let several children press small bits of green dough into the garlic press. When the dough comes out it will look like spaghetti. Have the children take the dough off the press and apply it to a section of moistened dough on the wreath. Continue pressing and applying the green dough until the top of the wreath is completely covered. Leave the center of each circle uncovered.

Press a candle into the center of each circle. The hole should be slightly larger than the candle to allow for shrinkage.

Let the children make red clay holly berries and secure them in groups of three to the top of the wreath.

Bake the wreaths at 300° for approximately two hours. When cool, spray the wreath with a clear polyurethane varnish to seal.

Put the candles in the wreath. Light the three purple candles the first weeks of Advent. The rose candle is lit the week before Christmas. On Christmas, light the white candle.

5. Winter

Suet-Seed Cups

Materials

several pounds of suet	double boiler
birdseed	wooden spoon
empty halves of oranges and grapefruit	hot plate or stove
medium-weight yarn	newspaper
needlepoint needles	

Preparation

Cut up suet and melt in the double boiler. Clean out the fruit.

Procedure

Make sure the citrus halves are fairly even across the top. Cut three pieces of yarn one-foot long and tie a knot in one end of each piece. Thread one length of yarn into the needle and stick the needle through a citrus half approximately one-half inch from the top edge. Attach two more pieces of yarn at equal distances away to form a triangle. Tie the yarn ends together. Set aside.

When the suet has melted and started boiling, pour in the birdseed to make a mixture the consistency of oatmeal. Cool slightly then melt again, stirring occasionally to keep it from burning. Take the mixture off the heat and quickly spoon it into the citrus halves. Cool. Use a freezer if one is available.

When the suet has cooled, hang the cups in a tree that can be seen from the classroom.

Once you begin feeding the birds, continue. The birds come to rely on the food which has been provided. Different classes can be responsible for bringing stale bread, cookies, birdseed, peanut butter, and suet each week until spring.

Shaking Snow Villages

Materials

small jars with screw-on lids	tablespoon
paraffin	small plastic figures
1 or 2 coffee cans or pots	moth ball flakes
colored and white felt squares	10″ of velveteen ribbon per child
glue	scissors

Preparation

Gather and clean enough small jars to have one per child. For each cut a circle from the colored felt the size of the lid and one smaller white circle. Skaters, snowmen, animals, little cabins, and trees are good examples of the figures you will need to buy for the snow villages.

Procedure

Melt the paraffin in an old coffee can or pot. Add a colored crayon. Keep the paraffin warm.

252

Each child will need to decide which of the figures he wants to use in his winter scenes. Let him experiment by placing the figures in the lid.

Pour a very thin layer of paraffin into the lid. Let the paraffin cool for about three minutes and then place the figures in it.

Fill the jars with water to within one inch of the top. Add one tablespoon of moth ball flakes to each jar. Have the children carefully screw on the tops of the jars. Make sure each jar lid is as tight as possible. Spread a thin layer of glue around each lid where it meets the glass jar. This will help to seal the lid.

Paste the colored felt circle to the top of the jar lid. Have each child fold a white felt circle in half three times. Use a pair of heavy scissors to cut out tiny triangles and to scallop the edge of the white circle. Be sure to have the children leave some of the areas along each of the folded sides intact so that the snowflake holds together. When finished, unfold the felt and glue the snowflake onto the colored felt circle.

The last step is to glue a length of ribbon around the outside edge of the jar lid.

The children will have fun tipping and shaking their snow villages. Remind the children not to unscrew the jar lids.

6. St. Valentine's Day

Bookmarks

Materials

1 3" × 3" square of white construction paper per child

1 2" × 2" square of red construction paper per child

1 7"× 1½" strip of white construction paper per child

1 7"×2" piece of red ribbon or red construction paper per child

blue felt-tip pens

scissors

heart patterns

glue

Preparation

Cut the squares and strips of paper to the required sizes. Cut out several patterns for two hearts. The large heart should be two and one-half inches tall and two and one-fourth inches wide. The smaller one should measure two inches tall by one and three-fourths inches wide. Gather the rest of the materials. Before class write a Scripture verse about love on a blackboard.

Procedure

Give each child a strip of white construction paper and a blue felt-tip pen and have him copy down the Scripture verse you have chosen. He should start approximately one inch from the top and write small.

When finished, give each child one red and one white square and have him trace around the heart patterns and cut hearts from the squares. To assemble the bookmark, glue the red heart to the center of the white heart. Glue the white strip onto the red strip of construction paper or ribbon. Glue the heart to the top of the bookmark.

Have each child take his bookmark home to give to a special person.

Cards

Materials

1 8″ × 10″ sheet of construction paper per child

sheets of red, pink, and white construction paper

doilies

old Valentine cards

paste

scraps of lace and ribbon

scissors

red, blue, or black felt-tip pens

Preparation

Give each child a large sheet of paper and tell him to fold it in half in either direction. Have the children plan how they want to make their cards. The cards may be made to look old-fashioned or very modern. Let the children use their imaginations. On the front of the card, have them write, "Trust in the Lord with all your heart, mind, and soul." On the inside, "For His love shall be with you always."

When the children are finished with the cards, have them sign them and give them to someone special.

Mailboxes

Materials

1 shoe box per child	pencils
1-2 rolls of butcher paper or white wrapping paper	transparent tape
	scraps of material, lace, and ribbon
red, pink, white, and blue construction paper	scissors
	paste
doilies	felt-tip pens
old Valentine cards	

Preparation

Send a note home the week before making the boxes, asking that each child bring a shoe box to class. Gather the other materials. Make up a sample box so that the children will be able to put cards for you in it.

Procedure

Demonstrate how to wrap the lid of the box separately from the body. Wrap both with white wrapping paper.

Have the children write their names on one end of their boxes.

The children should decide how they wish to decorate their mailboxes. Cut hearts out of paper or material. Lace, ribbon, doilies, and old valentines can be used to accent the boxes. Paste the decorations all over the box. Remind the children to leave a little room above their decorations on the body of the box for the lid. When finished, put the boxes in a place that has been designated as the post office.

The next week have the children bring Valentine cards for everyone in the class. Put some Valentine candy in the boxes ahead of time to surprise the children.

White lunch sacks can also be decorated and used for holding cards. The sacks can be tacked onto a bulletin board until the cards have been distributed.

7. St. Patrick's Day

Painted Clay Pots

Materials

1 3″ clay pot per child
1 bottle of Gesso
1 bottle of Mod Podge
¼ yd. of white material per child
1 yd. emerald green material
newspapers

1 shamrock plant per child
several patterns of four-leaf clovers
heavy scissors
paintbrushes
pie tins
potting soil

Preparation

Cut the white material into two-inch squares.

Make a pot to show as an example. Just before class cover the worktable with newspapers and fill several tins with Gesso. Fill several other tins with Mod Podge.

Procedure

The pots should be made the week before St. Patrick's Day and then planted the next week.

Give each child a pot and a paintbrush. Paint both the inside and outside with Gesso. The coat of Gesso should be fairly thick to seal the pores of the pot. When finished, clean the brushes well.

While the Gesso is drying, cut a large number of small four-leaf clovers from the green material. When the Gesso is dry, dip the squares of white material in the Mod Podge and then lay them on the outside of the pot. They should completely cover the pot, overlapping the edges of the material like a quilt. Dip the four-leaf clovers in Mod Podge and scatter them around the pot. When finished, paint a light coat of Mod Podge over the entire pot. The Mod Podge dries into a hard, clear surface.

The next week plant the shamrock plants in the pots. Shamrocks can usually be found at this time of year.

The children should keep the plants moist. When the shamrocks begin to grow tall trim them. This will help preserve their clover-like appearance.

8. Easter

Mosaic Butterfly Plaques

Materials

eggshells	polyurethane coating	food coloring	butterfly pattern
cotton swabs	sandpaper	black pipe cleaners	newspaper
pieces of wood	eye screws	small bowl of black	glue
stain	markers	tempera paint	

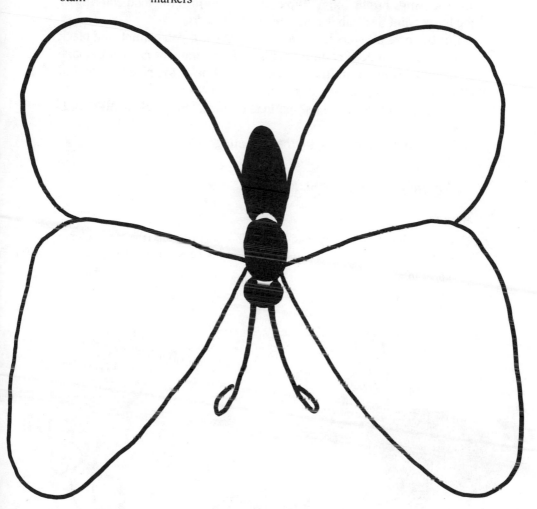

Procedure

Cut the wood into eight-and-one-half-by-eleven-inch pieces and sand the rough edges. Stain and let dry. Cut out the pattern and lay it on the wood so that the wood is turned lengthwise. Trace around the pattern and remove.

Crush the eggshells into medium-sized pieces. Put glue on the center of the butterfly. Place the crushed eggshells on the glue. Gently shake off the excess shells. Let dry.

Decide what colors you want your butterfly to be. Paint the center black and the wings bright colors. Dip cotton swabs into the food coloring or the black paint and dab it onto the shells. Let dry.

Cut the pipe cleaners into two-inch lengths. If you cannot find black pipe cleaners, you can paint them black. Bend one pipe cleaner to make an antenna. Run a thin line of glue on one side of the pipe cleaner and attach it to the top of the head.

At the top of the plaque use markers to print, "See, I Make All Things New."

Apply a thin layer of polyurethane coating.

Thumbprint Animal Stationery

Materials

white or colored stationery free of designs	colored felt-tip pens (the same color as the ink pads you are using)
envelopes to match the paper	1 practice sheet of paper per child
colored ink stamp pads	tissue paper and bows

Preparation

Gather the required materials. Use a practice sheet to experiment.

Procedure

Give each child a practice sheet and have him press a few thumbprints onto the paper. If he wants an animal to be standing, the thumbprint should be in an upright position. If he wants an animal to be lying down or crouching, the thumbprint should be in a horizontal position. The faces, ears, tails, legs, etc. can be drawn with a pen. Trees, bushes, and grasses can also be drawn. A few examples of animals which can easily be created from thumbprints are: rabbits, kangaroos, mice, bees, butterflies, squirrels, fish, and turtles.

When ready to make the stationery, give each child ten sheets of paper and have him make a scene with one or two animals in the top left corner. Then give each child ten envelopes and have him put a small animal in the lower left corner or on the back flap.

Wrap the stationery in tissue paper and tie on a pretty bow. This would be an excellent present for a grandmother, mother, or a friend.

Picture Frame Pencil Holders

Materials

construction paper	tin cans 2½" in diameter
scissors	wallet-size pictures of Jesus

Procedure

Cut the construction paper into eight-by-ten-inch sheets. Fold the paper in half lengthwise and then unfold to make a center crease. Fold the top and the bottom over until they meet at the center crease. Turn back the edges on the top layer of paper to form a triangle at each corner. Slip one end into the other. Place the picture of Jesus into the center and slip the frame over a tin can.

Matchstick Crosses

Materials

small stick matches
poster board or plywood
glue

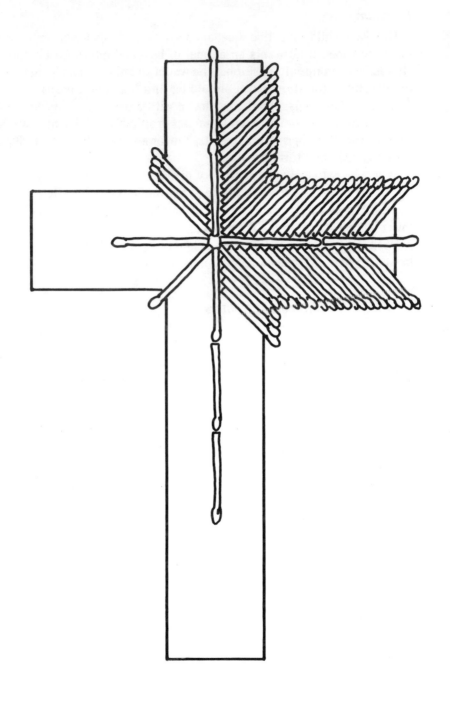

Preparation

Burn the ends of the matches. (Do this outside to vent the sulfur smell.) Rub the burnt ends gently to remove the black ash.

Procedure

Cut a cross out of poster board so that it is slightly shorter than two matches end on end. The ends of the matches will extend beyond the edges of the poster board.

Glue four matches in the center of the poster board to form a cross. Glue four more matches on the cross with the burned ends outward to form an eight-point star at the center of the cross. Continue to fill in the cross with matches laid burned ends turned outward and projecting beyond the edges of the poster board or plywood.

9. Spring

Suncatcher Animals

Materials

book of animal stencils	scissors
black construction paper	pencils
rolls of cellophane	nylon thread
glue	

Procedure

Decide what type of animal you want to make. Fold a piece of black construction paper in half and trace the animal. Cut out the silhouettes. With a pencil draw a line one-quarter inch from the outside edge all the way around the animal. Carefully cut out the inside. Repeat this process so that you have two identical silhouettes.

Cut a piece of cellophane and put glue all over the outline of one of the animals. Place the cellophane on top of the outline and then glue the second outline on top. Be sure to line them up exactly. Cut off the excess cellophane.

Punch a small hole in the top of the animal and run a piece of nylon thread through it. Tie the ends and use this as a hanger.

Eggshell Pictures

Materials

2 4″ × 3″ squares of plywood per child   scissors
1 can of light-colored spray paint   glue
eggshells   picture hangers
2 small pictures of flowers or animals   newspapers
shellac or clear acrylic spray

Preparation

Cut the small wood plaques. Spray paint all sides of the plaques with two coats of paint.

Buy the pictures needed from a craft store. The pictures may be colorful flowers, cuddly animals, or something that represents spring. The pictures should be approximately two or two and one-half inches tall.

Gather the rest of the materials.

Procedure

Have the children each choose two pictures from the selection you have available. Center the pictures on the plaques and glue down.

Crush the eggshells into tiny pieces. Cover the area around the pictures with glue and sprinkle the eggshells on top of the glue. Pat the eggshells down to make sure they adhere.

Spray the plaques with two or three coats of fixative spray.

Attach a picture hanger to the back of each picture.

Spring Wrapping Paper

Materials

several packets of white tissue paper   newspapers
½ potato per child   brown and green felt-tip markers (optional)
paring knives
thick pink tempera paint in shallow   paint shirts
bowls   pencils

Preparation

Gather the required materials. Set up a work area and a drying area.

Procedure

Show the children a picture or drawing of a cherry blossom. Give each a potato half. Have him draw a cherry blossom on the potato. Cut away all areas of the potato which surround the flower. The flower should sit approximately one-half inch above the rest of the potato.

Give each child two sheets of tissue paper. Lay the sheets directly on top of each other. To print, dip the potato lightly into pink paint and then press it onto the tissue paper. Print the flowers randomly over the entire sheet of paper. Lay the paper on the floor to dry.

Several sheets of wrapping paper can be made by each child.

Save the wrapping paper to wrap presents.

10. Pentecost

Dove Key Holders

Materials

dove pattern	newspaper
¼" plywood	nail
wood stain or paint	small hooks
brushes	jigsaw

Preparation

Cut one dove per child from plywood, using a jigsaw.

Procedure

Lay newspaper on the work area and stain or paint the doves. Let dry.

With a nail start small holes across the body of the dove. Once the holes are started you will be able to screw in the small hooks. Put one of the hooks in the center of the top wing and use it to hang up the key holder.

Kites

Materials

large pieces of butcher paper

flat dowels

markers

heavy string

glue or stapler

crepe paper or long strips of light-weight material

Procedure

Cut the paper into a diamond shape. Use markers to decorate both sides of the paper.

Fold under one inch on all sides. Cut away one inch of paper on each corner (see diagram). On the inside of the fold run a line of glue all the way around the kite. Lay the string along the glue and fold over the one inch of paper. Make sure you have a continuous string all the way around, leaving a little slack at the cut-out sections.

Cut the dowels to fit across the kite with about one-quarter inch excess. Cut a slit in the end of each dowel. Tie the dowels together where they meet. Fit the string into the slits in the dowels where you have cut out the corners.

Make a tail out of crepe paper or material. Staple in place.

Tie the end of a ball of string to the middle of the backside where the dowels cross.

11. Gifts

Memory Boxes

Materials

4" square styrofoam containers (Use the kind into which fast food restaurants put sandwiches.)

brown or a bright color of tempera paint

2 picture hangers per child

modeling compound, bread clay, or glue dough

acrylic paint

glue

oilcloth for worktable

scissors

rulers

small brushes

waxed paper

newspapers

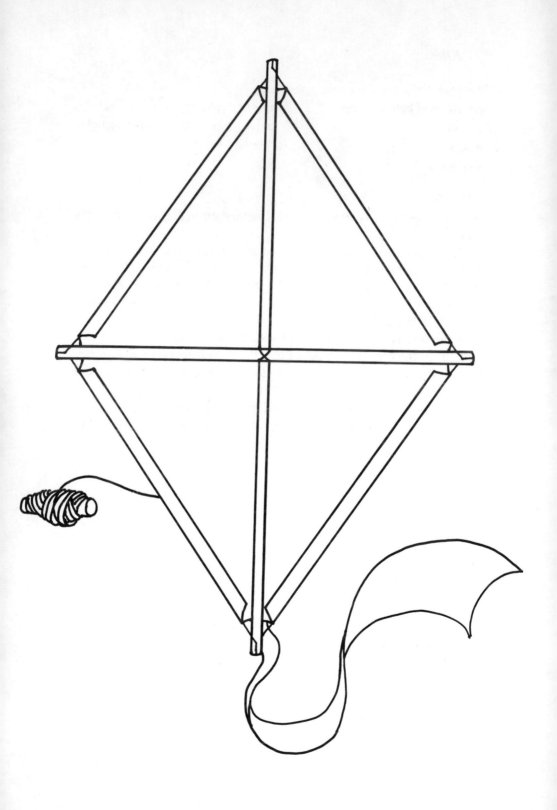

Preparation

Mix bread clay or glue dough according to the recipes found in Recipes and Methods at the back of the book.

Make several figures as examples.

Procedure

Work on the figures first. Three-dimensional reliefs may be made of such figures as bread and a wine chalice, angels, doves, praying hands, crosses, or any other religious symbol. Or make figures such as flowers, animals, strawberries, or mushrooms. Let the children decide what they want to make and give them time to experiment. Each child will make two boxes.

The figures should be no larger than three inches square and between one-half and one inch thick. If using bread clay or glue dough the figures should be placed on waxed paper and left to dry for two days. Modeling compound should be baked and cooled.

Cut the styrofoam boxes in half and trim off the locking edges. Paint the inside and outside of each of the boxes with tempera paint. (Do not use spray paint.) When the paint is dry, glue on picture hangers. Mark the child's initials on the back of his boxes.

Paint the clay figures and let dry thoroughly. The figures may be attached to the inside of the boxes with glue. Let the glue dry before picking up the boxes.

Have each child wrap the memory boxes in colored tissue paper and give them to his mother, grandmother, or to a special person.

Jewelry Boxes

Materials

1 plastic quart-size bleach bottle or liquid dish detergent bottle per child

X-Acto knives or sharp kitchen scissors

1 yd. of colorful calico material

rickrack or braid coordinated to go with the material

sewing scissors

pencils

tacky glue

rulers

Preparation

Send notes home the week before doing this project, asking that each child bring a plastic quart-size bottle. It should be empty and clean.

Gather the rest of the materials.

Procedure

Have each child mark a line across the bottle approximately two inches up from the bottom. Use an X-Acto knife or scissors to cut off the bottom of each bottle.

Measure the amount of material needed to cover the sides of the

bottles. A little extra is needed for covering the top edge of the bottle. Glue the material to the sides of the bottle, covering the top edge of the container. Measure and glue rickrack to the top edge of the container and then around the container, approximately one inch from the first line of rickrack. Glue a line of rickrack to the inside to cover the edge of the material. Let the glue dry.

Wrap the jewelry boxes in colorful tissue paper. Have the children give the boxes to their mothers.

To make a catchall for a father, use a solid color of material or spray paint the bottle. Then use a coordinating color of tape to cover the top edge of the bottle. Paste appropriate pictures on the sides.

Embroidered Sachets

(A two-week lesson)

Materials

1 6" × 6" square of medium-weave cotton or linen per child

1 small embroidery hoop per child

1 packet of embroidery patterns

several colors of embroidery floss

embroidery needles

1 bag of polyester fiberfill

embroidery scissors

perfumed powder

Preparation

Buy light-colored material which can be embroidered easily. Cut the material into six-inch squares. Embroidery hoops and other embroidery supplies can be found in a craft or sewing supply store.

Print a pattern on each piece of material. The patterns should be centered.

Procedure

Demonstrate the basic embroidery stitches which may be used. You will probably want to show them how to make the satin stitch, long and short stitch, and an outlining stitch. Those who have had experience embroidering may also learn the lazy daisy stitch and the French knot. Refer to a basic stitch book for the directions.

Give each child a piece of material with the pattern of his choice. Show him how to secure the material in the embroidery hoop. Then let him start embroidering the pattern with embroidery floss. Use a two-ply strand (two of the individual threads) about twelve inches long. Tie a double knot at the beginning and when he is finished with the thread.

When the entire pattern has been outlined and/or filled in, fold the right sides together and stitch across both ends of the packet with small stitches which run close together. There should be an opening in the center of the back. Turn the right side out and fill with the stuffing material. Sprinkle powder in the sachet. Use an overlapping stitch to close the center seam of the packet.

Wrap the sachets. The sachets can be given to a mother, grandmother, aunt, or to a favorite teacher.

PART 4

Recipes and Methods

1. Papier-mâché

Procedure

Papier-mâché is a method of paper sculpture accomplished by dipping strips of paper in paste and applying to a basic form. Piñatas, hats, bracelets, animal and people figures, and many other objects can be created with papier-mâché.

Put one cup flour in a small bowl and gradually add one cup warm water until the paste has the consistency of cream soup. The paste may be kept in a sealed container and refrigerated for several days without spoiling.

Wallpaper paste also works well. Just follow the package directions.

The paste may take several days to dry. You may paint your sculpture when dry and later coat with polyurethane spray for a shiny, waterproof finish.

2. Frosting Paint

Materials

2 or 3 tbs. margarine	2 or 3 tbs. milk
2 c. confectioner's sugar	food coloring

Procedure

Cream confectioner's sugar and margarine. Gradually beat in milk to make a fluffy frosting. Divide frosting into smaller bowls and add food coloring to make desired colors.

White frosting mix made according to package directions works just as well.

3. Pudding Paint

Materials

1 3 oz. pkg. instant pudding mix

2 c. cold milk

Procedure

Mix the pudding as directed on package. Refrigerate for about one-half hour until thick.

Use pudding paint the same way you use finger paint.

4. Soapsuds Paint

Materials

2-3 tbs. powdered tempera paint per
color

2-3 tbs. liquid dish detergent per color

1 tbs. liquid starch per color

small amount of water

Procedure

Combine all ingredients in a small bowl, using just enough water to make the paint syrupy. Beat paint with an eggbeater or wisk until thick and puffy.

Store paint in covered jars. Whip to reactivate.

Use soapsuds paint on a fairly water-resistant surface as the paint will bleed. Allow two hours drying time.

5. Glue Dough*

Materials

1 part Elmer's Glue

1 part corn starch

1 part white flour

food coloring

* Recipe created by the Borden Chemical Division of Borden, Inc., makers of Elmer's Glue. Taken from *Fun Projects* pamphlet, copyright 1979.

Procedure

Place equal amounts of glue, corn starch, and flour in bowl. Add food coloring. Mix until ingredients form a ball. Knead dough until pliable. Add more flour if dough is too moist; add more glue if dough is too dry. Store in plastic bags.

Use glue dough like you use clay or bread dough. Allow twenty-four hours drying time (no baking necessary).

6. Bread Dough for Sculptures

Materials

2 c. all-purpose flour

1 c. salt

1 c. water

Procedure

Combine flour and salt in a large bowl. Add water, a little at a time, mixing until the dough particles begin to adhere to each other. The dough should be similar in texture to pie crust dough. (The amount of water needed varies according to the humidity in the air. On very dry days you may need more than one cup of water. If the dough seems sticky, add more flour.) Form several balls. Knead the dough for seven to ten minutes until smooth and firm. Store in plastic bags to prevent drying. Refrigerate. Dough should be kept no more than five days.

Do not double this recipe. In large batches the dough is hard to handle and will not hold together well.

Most dough sculptures, such as Christmas tree ornaments and baskets, begin with a base of flat, rolled dough. Roll out a small portion of dough and cut the base figures. Decorate them by adding bits of bread dough. These common tools can be used to make different effects: forks, butter knives, spoons, garlic presses, holiday cookie cutters, candles, candy and cake molds, toothpicks, and clay modeling tools.

When working with the dough, always have your hands and work surface floured. This helps to keep the dough from sticking. When using cookie cutters or molds, cover with a light coat of cooking oil to prevent the dough from sticking.

To attach two pieces of bread dough together, moisten both edges with water and press together. The water acts as a bonding material and helps to keep the pieces together during the baking stage.

There are two ways of hardening dough sculptures. The first is to let the dough dry in the air. This method is slower than using an oven, but the dough will dry just as hard. Put the sculpture on a screen and prop it up on two containers so that the air will circulate freely on all sides. It takes approximately forty-eight hours to dry a piece this way. Air drying is not recommended for very thick sculptures.

The other method is to bake the sculpture in an oven at 300°F. Let the dough bake one-half hour per one-fourth inch of thickness or until the outside of the sculpture is golden brown. Set the sculpture on a foil-lined cookie sheet to bake. Bake the dough sculptures as soon as you can after making them; otherwise finer pieces may crumble. If the sculptures begin to puff up, reduce the oven temperature by approximately 50° and poke a hole in the puffed area with a pin. Extremely thin pieces bake more rapidly. Keep an eye on them so they do not burn. If cracking should occur, remove the sculpture from the oven, fill the crack with moistened dough and then put it back in the oven at a slightly lower temperature.

There are several ways to finish dough sculptures. The most common one is to paint the sculpture with an egg-milk mixture about fifteen minutes after you have started baking it. Then return it to the oven. If you want a dark brown finish, repeat the painting process every ten to fifteen minutes until the sculpture is finished. Varnish the sculpture when it has completely cooled.

The other method is to paint the sculpture with acrylic paint. This usually requires two coats of paint. No varnish is required since the paint will seal the sculpture.

7. Salt Dough

Materials

⅔ c. salt

⅓ c. water

½ c. flour

food coloring or tempera paint

Procedure

Measure salt, flour, and water into a large mixing bowl. If you do not add food coloring or tempera paint, the beads or objects made will be very white. To make colored beads, add a few drops of food coloring or tempera paint to the water. Mix well. Store in plastic bags and refrigerate up to two months.

When ready to use, roll a small amount of clay between the palms of your hands to make a small ball or roll. The small balls can be made into round beads. If flattened, they can be cut to form triangular or square beads. Before letting the beads dry, a hole should be made in the center of each with a toothpick. The rolls can be braided or fashioned into items with straight or curved lines.

The dough should be baked in a slow oven (200°F) for about two hours or left out overnight to dry.

8. Finger Paint

Materials

1 c. laundry starch	½ c. salt
2 tbs. corn starch	3 c. warm water
cold water	food coloring or dry tempera paint
1 c. soap flakes	1 tsp. glycerin (optional)

Procedure

Mix the laundry starch, corn starch, and a small amount of cold water to make a smooth paste. Add the soap flakes and salt. Mix until smooth. Put this mixture in a double boiler and add warm water, a little at a time, cooking slowly until thick. Add glycerin and beat with an eggbeater or mixer. Divide the mixture into baby food jars. Add several drops of food coloring or dry tempera paint to make desired colors. You may have to add more water if you use tempera paint.

This recipe makes enough paint for approximately thirty pictures. Make the finger paint before class and refrigerate. It will keep for a week or more without spoiling.

9. Bread Clay

(Makes twelve one-inch balls.)

Materials

4 large slices white bread
4 tbs. white glue
1 tsp. glycerin or clear liquid detergent (softening ingredient)
corn starch
acrylic paints

Procedure

Remove crusts from bread and shread the remaining bread into fine pieces. Place in a bowl and add white glue and glycerin. The clay can be whitened by adding a few drops of white paint or colored by adding drops of colored paint. Sprinkle the work area with corn starch and also lightly dust the palms of your hands. Knead the bread mixture until it forms a pliable clay. Roll the clay into several balls and store in plastic bags.

When working with the clay, keep your hands moistened with hand lotion. If the clay becomes too dry add a few drops of the softening ingredient and knead the clay until it is pliable. If the clay is too sticky, dust the clay with corn starch and knead again. Use only a little clay at a time. Keep the rest in a plastic bag to maintain the suitable moisture level.

The clay will take about two days to dry thoroughly. When a clay figure is completed, it should be brushed with two light coats of thinned white glue. (Dilute one part glue with one part water.) This will prevent the clay from cracking. Allow the first coat to dry before applying the second coat. The dried figure may be painted with acrylic paint.

Bread clay may be used to make flowers, animals, tiny dolls, angels, fruit, or anything else that can be molded from clay.

10. Name Tags

Procedure

Make simple name tags with no pins to injure the wearer by using a spring-hinged clothespin. Print the person's name on the flat surface of the clothespin and clip it to the front of the wearer's shirt, pocket, or collar.

11. Flannel Board and Figures

Board

Materials

1 large appliance box
1 to 2 yards of light-colored flannel
transparent tape
1 to 2 yards of colorful contact paper

Procedure

Cut the appliance box apart, leaving one of the corners intact. This will allow you to fold the board for convenient storage. Cover the cardboard base with flannel. Use contact paper to cover the back and to secure the flannel to the cardboard. Cover one to two inches of the material with contact paper. Attach supports to the back of the board with tape.

Now you have a flannel board that can be put on an easel or can stand on a table by itself. When folded, it can easily be stored on a shelf with your flannel board figures.

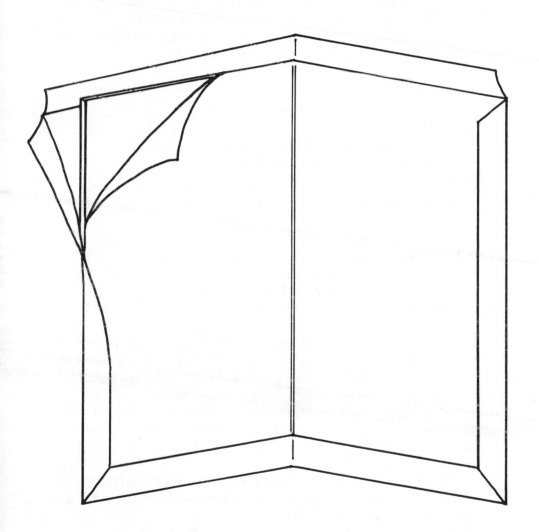

Figures

Materials

1 yd. of heavyweight Pellon
1 black felt-tip pen
crayons
coloring books with the figures you desire

Procedure

Choose your figures from a coloring book or picture book and lay the Pellon over the book. Using a black felt-tip pen, trace around the figure and add facial features and clothing. On the shiny side of the Pellon, color the figures with crayons. The rough side will adhere to the flannel. Cut them from the Pellon and they are ready to use.

12. Puppet Stage

Materials

very large cardboard box (Refrigerator boxes work well.)
knife
contact paper or paint
brushes
heavy yarn
different colors of plain material
brads (brass paper fastener)

Procedure

Refrigerator boxes usually come with removable tops. Remove the top but do not discard. Using a knife, cut a square hole in the front side for the stage. Cut off the back from the box and discard.

If you want to paint the box, lay newspaper below it and paint any color. Let dry.

If you use contact paper, measure and cut the lengths you will need. Peel off the backing and stick to the box making sure that you remove all air bubbles. This method will cost more but will last longer and look nicer.

Put a brad about halfway back on each side of the box to use for securing the curtains. Separate the brads on the outside but don't make them too tight. Make curtains with a casing at the top. Run yarn through the casing and tie the ends around the brads. Put tape across the brads to secure. Bend the brads tight.

When using the stage, the children will sit on the floor. The curtain serves as a background and the show is performed through the large square in front of it. (See diagram.)

278

FRONT

BACK

13. Bartholomew, the Birthday Caterpillar

This wall decoration makes it easy to keep track of the children's birthdays as they occur throughout the year.

Materials

13 12" to 15" circles of light-colored construction paper. You will need one for each month of the year and one for the head of the caterpillar.

black felt-tip pen

transparent tape

Procedure

Trace around a dinner plate or large mixing bowl to make thirteen construction paper circles. Save the scraps of paper to cut out small horns for the caterpillar.

Draw a happy face on the caterpillar and attach the horns. Outline the circle with a black felt-tip marker. Label the other circles with the names of the months. Outline these circles, too. Attach the circles together, starting with the first month of the school year.

Write in the names and birthdates of the children who have birthdays during each month. Add to it as new children join your class.

Hang Bartholomew in a prominent place to help you and the children remember birthdays.

14. Scratch Method

The scratch method may be used for many types of pictures, especially those with fine details. A lesson depicting the fall of the walls of Jericho, Noah's ark landing on Mount Ararat, and a scary Halloween night are excellent examples of where fine detail may be added.

Materials

1 sheet of heavy construction paper or tagboard per child

crayons

brushes

scratching tools: nails, bobby pins, paper clips, forks, etc.

newspapers

India ink or thick tempera paint

paint shirts

Procedure

Have the children color very heavily with an assortment of crayons. Cover the entire page or block the paper into different squares of color. Then paint the paper with India ink or tempera paint. Let the ink or paint dry.

When ready, have the children lightly draw their picture to determine placement. Use the various scratching tools to put in details. Scratch lightly enough to take off only the layer of paint. The color will show through.

15. Wet Chalk Method

By drawing on wet construction paper with pastel chalks, the colors will bleed and give a fuzzy or watery appearance. This method is particularly effective when doing scenes which include water. Eerie Halloween scenes or winter snow pictures also can be done effectively by this method.

Procedure

Wet the construction paper by rubbing over it lightly with a damp sponge.

Draw your picture with pastel chalk. Do not press too hard or the paper will tear. The colors will bleed on each side of the lines that have been drawn. Rub the chalk with a finger to spread any color desired. Continue until the picture is finished. If necessary, dampen the paper again. If you wish to have an area with more detail, leave this until last.

16. Soap Carving

Materials

1 large bar of soap per child (Green soap is good for turtles, lizards, and frogs. Yellow soap is good for lions and cats. Fish, doves, bunnies, and houses can be made from white soap.)

1 paring knife per child

acrylic paints

turpentine

pencils

small brushes

Procedure

Give each child a bar of soap and a knife. Scrape off the lettering on the top of the soap. While doing this the children should be thinking of the best way their sculpture will fit on the soap. Most animals are best made sitting or standing, with the soap standing on a long side. A turtle can be made by laying the bar of soap flat and working from the head down to the feet. Houses and other buildings can be made by laying several bars of soap in different directions.

Each child should draw a basic outline on the bar of soap. Features such as heads, tails, feet, and so forth need to be drawn roughly, so that the children will not forget to carve them as well.

Carefully cut away the outside of the basic outline. Cut out fine details last. Always remember to leave a little room for error.

PART 5

Musical Instruments

1. Shakers

Materials

styrofoam cups
dried peas or beans
masking tape
markers

Procedure

Put the beans or peas in a cup. Put another cup on top of the one holding the peas so that the wide ends are together. Run several strips of masking tape completely around the middle of the shaker where the two cups join. Use markers to decorate the outside of the cups.

2. Sandpaper Blocks

Materials

small blocks of scrap lumber
sandpaper
glue
spray paint (optional)

Procedure

Sand the edges of the wood. Paint the block if desired. Cut sandpaper to fit one side of the block and glue it in place.

To play, clap two blocks together and gently rub in a rhythmic manner.

You may have to peel off the sandpaper and replace it or glue another piece over the first after the sandpaper is worn.

3. Tambourines

Materials

paper plates
bottle caps
stapler
marker or crayons

Procedure

Put two plates face to face. Staple around the edges, putting the staples very close together. Leave a two-inch gap. Insert the bottle caps. Finish stapling. Use markers to decorate the outside.

To play, hold in one hand and hit with the palm of the other hand in time to the music.

Bell Tambourines

Materials

paper plates   markers
small bells   pipe cleaners
paper punch

Procedure

Color the back sides of two paper plates.

Punch holes around the outside about one inch from the edge and about three inches apart. To make sure you can align the holes, put the plates together and punch the two plates at the same time.

Cut the pipe cleaners into three-inch lengths. Put one end through one of the holes and thread on a bell. Twist the ends together to secure. Continue in this manner until all the bells are around the plates.

To play, hold in one hand and gently hit with the palm of the other hand in time to the music.

4. Drums

Materials

oatmeal boxes   scrap pieces of leather
brown construction paper   leather shoestrings
markers   paper punch

Procedure

Cover the outside of the oatmeal box with brown construction paper. Decorate with markers.

Cover the top and the bottom with leather which is cut two to three inches larger than the top so that it can be pulled over the sides. Punch holes all the way around the edge of the leather pieces one inch from the edge and one inch apart. Place one of the pieces of leather on the table and set the container on top of it. Place the other piece of leather on the top. With the leather shoestrings lace from the top to the bottom, pulling the leather taut. Tie the ends together securely when you have finished.

5. Kazoos

Materials

cardboard tubes   rubber bands
waxed paper   markers or paint

Procedure

Use any size cardboard tubes from wrapping paper, toilet tissue, foil, etc. Cut long tubes to make three or four kazoos.

Paint the tubes or use markers to decorate them.

Cut a piece of waxed paper large enough to wrap around one end of the tube. Secure with a rubber band.

Punch a hole about two inches from the covered end.

To play, hum into the open end of the tube.

6. Rhythm Sticks

Materials

dowels at least ½" in diameter and 12" long
spray or acrylic paint
newspaper

Procedure

Cover the work area with newspaper. Use spray paint or acrylic paint to cover the dowels. Markers or other colors of paint may be used to make designs on the dowels when the paint is dry.

To play, hold a stick in each hand and tap one on the other in time to the music.

7. Jingle Bell Sticks

Materials

dowels at least ½" in diameter and 12" long

small bells

spray paint

heavy yarn

stapler

newspaper

Procedure

Lay newspaper on the work area. Spray paint the dowels.

String two inches of heavy yarn through each bell. Anchor each with a knot. Staple the ends of the yarn to the dowel. Put eight to ten bells on one end of each stick.

To play, shake the sticks or strike two together.

8. Wrist Bells

Materials

5" strips of wide elastic

small bells

crewel needles

yarn

Preparation

Sew the ends of the elastic together using a sewing machine.

Procedure

Thread the needle with yarn. Tie a knot in the end. Start at the underside of the elastic and come through to the top. Thread through the bell and back down through the elastic. Continue sewing until all the bells are around the elastic. Knot the end when the last bell is attached.

To play, slip the elastic over the wrist and shake.

9. Cymbals

Materials

2 aluminum pie plates

empty wooden spools

wood putty

nail

Procedure

Fill the middle of a spool with wood putty and let dry. Stand the spool on a hard surface. Lay a pie pan face down on top of the spool. Hammer the nail through the pie pan into the spool.

To play, hold one cymbal in each hand and clap together in time to the music.

10. Papier-mâché Maracas

Materials

small balloons	½" dowels 5" long
strips of newspaper	paint and brushes
flour	paint shirts
salt	straight pins
water	dried peas or small BBs

Procedure

Blow up a balloon.

In a large container mix two cups of flour, one-half cup salt and enough water to make a soupy paste.

Dip the newspaper into the flour mixture and wrap around the balloon. Cover the balloon with several layers, leaving a small hole in the bottom. Let dry.

Use a straight pin to pop the balloon. Insert BBs or peas through the hole and place the dowel into the hole, leaving a three-inch handle. Seal the hole with more of the papier-mâché or with masking tape. Paint the maraca one color. Let dry and then paint or use markers to add designs or flowers.

To play, shake in time to the music.